Lily Siou

氣功八段錦

曾克耑署

Ch'i Kung

強行者有志
不失其所者久
死而不忘者壽

道德經

不若智自天者明
勝人者有力自勝者強
不若蓋章田

Ch'i Kung
The Art of Mastering
the Unseen Life Force

Lily Siou, Ph. D.

CHARLES E. TUTTLE COMPANY
Rutland, Vermont

REPRESENTATIVES

Continental Europe:
  BOXERBOOKS, INC., Zurich

British Isles:
  PRENTICE-HALL INTERNATIONAL, INC., London

Australasia:
  BOOK WISE, BEVERLY, SOUTH AUSTRALIA

Published by The Charles E. Tuttle Co., Inc.
Rutland, Vermont

Library of Congress Card Number: 75-32212
International Standard Book Number 0-8048-1169-5

First printed in 1973
by Lily Siou's School of the Six Chinese Arts
First Tuttle printing, 1975
Second Tuttle printing, 1981
Third Tuttle printing, 1984
Fourth Tuttle printing, 1987

Printed in U.S.A.

Preface

At the dawn of mankind, primitive man lived a very simple life. His main concern then was physical survival. His daily task was to fight for food and to survive against nature, enemy and beast. He lived on a very physical level. Through his struggles to survive, he developed fitness and prowess. Fitness and prowess in turn brought survival.

This simple fact of nature forced itself upon the consciousness of man everywhere. Through time, however, the importance of this fact was lessened by changes in the conditions of man. With the cultivation of crops and domestication of beasts, less was the need for direct physical contest against death. Countless changes too in technology and social conditions have brought man to where he is today-in cities, in environments quite distant from nature, in conditions which even require him to sublimate expression and agressive energies. The too often realities – tension, anxiety, highblood pressure, obesity and loss of vigor – extensive deconditionging.

Direct physical exertion of the individual parts through exercise has been the primary means of combating deconditioning in the West. But exercise that requires exertion is tiring and requires much determination and effort. It requires quite the opposite of what most people are inclined to put forth especially when tired. Also, exercise in the West are, as a rule, dissectory and specific. It is usually limited to just physical development of a very specific muscle or set of muscles without regard to benifitting the body as a whole and without attention to the person as a whole being.

Going back again to early man, we see that the Chinese remained very close to nature. They were ever conscious of things being part of a system in a web of relationships. They had no hesitation in relating what they saw in nature to their own situation. Studying the movements of animals, he had no trouble relating their movements to his own. He was aware of the differences between man and animal but he was able to obtain from animal movements certain valuable features. By study and practice he was able to adapt these features to his own needs and improve upon them. He remained, throughout, ever conscious of a prevading system of forces, the wholeness and universal relatedness of things.

This has its importance when we contrast it to western relish for isolating problem and solution from its total circumstances under the urgency for a solution. The westerner sees exercise as exercise, dance as dance and emotion as something just emotional. He is predisposed to seeing things as units or as a collection of seperate units. He is goal oriented and he prefers simplified solutions. Even for his own garden, he is more likely to construct his walkway in a straight path than to let it meander around brook and stone. He is satisfied if "it works", and in mathematics, he honors a simple solution with the term "elegant".

One can indeed say that the simplest solution in mathematics is elegant, but the problems of man can rarely enjoy the luxury of being in a closed system as mathematics. Most problems of man involve many disciplines and demand a concern for totality. To ignore this fact is to invite other problems. Man's threatened environment and growing social ills result from his preoccupation with technology and industrialization. There are real benefits in considering a problem and its solutions in relationship to other factors. On the individual level, he is learning that treatment of emotional problems cannot be confined to treating just the emotions. He must look to the physical and beyond. Hence the terms psycho-physical, psychosomatic and psycho-social.

Health, fitness and emotion go together. Why should exercise be for exercise only, dance for dance only and emotional therapy for emotional therapy only? Can one not improve the health, gain vigor, fitness and tranquility in one effort?

The ancient Chinese lived with nature and saw that nature had its own way — a way which existed long before man and which would continue long after him. He realized very early, that he must accept and work with this way. To oppose the way was foolish. To follow the way was wise. Little effort is needed when one heeds the way. "Nature has a wisdom we know not yet of", but by listening very closely we may learn of its ways.

While the West focused its attention upon the external, the East focused on the internal. Both East and West advanced very far in their opposite study. The Chinese listened very closely to the needs and ways of the body and developed a unique understanding to it — an understanding which enables remarkable control and usage. Chinese martial arts is one example. Summing up strength and releasing it in a sudden smashing blow may seem remarkable to westerners but represent a tiny fraction of what is possible. More sophisticated are the soft styles of physical discipline which do not rely on strength but body mechanics. In these arts, each form, each movement is efficient. There is little waste of either movement or energy because attention is paid to the total body and the total situation. Not only is ones own body used with maximum efficiency, but the enemy's power is diverted and turned against himself.

The Chinese have developed, too, even subtler control of the body in a unique, and seldom heard of art called Ch'i Kung. In this art they generate and control the body energy and achieve a profound mastery of the body.

In Ch'i Kung the same Ch'i or life energy that acupuncturists stimulate and control through needles is mastered but to an even higher degree. In fact, acupuncture is merely a short cut in the application of this larger study. In this art even the minutest mechanisms such as oxygen level, blood supply, heart rate, blood pressure, body temperature, anti-body level can be controlled. Organ function is stimulated and inter-organ blance is achieved to bring about optimum overall health and a sense of overall harmony and well being.

This art still survives today, but few know much more about it than its existence. Fewer yet can be called masters. Lily Siou is such a master. At nine, in Kiangsi Province, China, she became a disciple of the Taoist. Through years of discipleship there, through long continued personal working experience with Ch'i and the related arts of I Ching, palmistry, face reading, chinese medicine and acupuncture, she has gained an intimate knowledge of this lifes energy "Ch'i" and of Ch'i Kung Later in Hong Kong she attended the Hong Kong Chinese University and earned degrees in two fields and later a Ph. D. for her work on the I Ching.

Dr. Lily Siou, now 26, is the authoress of four books in Chinese and two others to be published in English soon, These two in English include a handbook on acupuncture and the most thorough and definitive work yet on the ancient classic, the I Ching. Dr. Siou, a former dean at the Hong Kong Christian College, left Hong Kong three years ago to test her theories in the western world. In that time too she established a school in the United States to keep alive this important ancient art of Ch'i Kung which is virtually unknown in the West and presently faces extinction in China. Chi Kung deserves preservation for its historic and cultural value but more importantly for the benefits that it offers mankind.

Professor Tseng Ke-tuan
Poet Laureate, Dean of Arts and Letters
Chinese University of Hong Kong

Authoress'es Forword

Through the ages, the Chinese have developed many valuable arts and practices. However, through the course of time, some of these arts have been completely or partially lost to the modern world, leaving behind often times, only their Chinese characters and a vague idea of what it was. Ch'i Kung is one example. Ch'i Kung an ancient but profound body and mind discipline embodying much of Chinese philosophy was once a subject of much study in China. Boxers of the Wei Dynasty firmly upheld that systematic breathing control, Ch'i Kung, led to better Kung Fu. Ch'i Kung is believed to be responsible for the brilliant and active developement of Chinese martial arts at this time. But today it survives mainly through the practice of a very few. Books on Ch'i Kung are only a handful. The Library of Congress reports that there is no work on Ch'i Kung in English. Even in Chinese there is little on the subject, just bits and pieces of material or very small books on it. In writing about Ch'i Kung, therefore, I am forced to rely largely on my knowledge and understanding about it gained through my years of study with the Taoist monks. I hope that this book as a first seed in the Western world will grow and flourish for the benifit of all. Through it, I hope to show the way to better health and well being through the natural movements of Ch'i Kung and to further the understanding of philosophies of the East and West. Through my School of the Six Chinese Arts, I hope to do the same.

In the summer of 1970, I brought four books written by myself into the Western world with the hope that they could be of some use here. These books were on the I Ching, Chinese herbs, acupuncture and cauterization and on Ch'i Kung. These works have aided me in my lectures and should be of interest to anyone curious about the Chinese.

It is this last book together with the works of Hua T'o that have constituted the major literary resources available. Hua T'o of the Three Kingdoms, one of the greatest physicians of all times was the first exponent of systematic exercises and Ch'i Kung. He developed a systematic exercise called the "Playing of the Five Animals" (五 離 戲   ).

Most of his works were destroyed by time and what have been handed down to the present are only two books on the subject. On is called PA TUEN CHIN (八 段 錦   ) meaning "eight precious chapters" and it is translated into the Eight Silken Forms. The other is called I CHING CHING (易 筋 經   ) meaning "the canon of the changing muscles". Many books mention and refer to Ch'i Kung but these are about all the books there are on Ch'i Kung in Chinese.

In writing this work, I owe much to many people. Many teachers, doctors, friends and students assisted me in completing the work for publication. I would like to acknowledge Dr. C. C. Hu, M. D., Kiangsi Province Divisional Hospital, China, for many valuable ideas gained from his lectures. As literary advisors on the theory and philosophy of Ch'i Kung and the inter-relationship of the yin and the yang, I would like to thank former professor I Ju Chen of St. John's University of Shanghai, Professor Ke-Tuan Tseng of the Chinese University of Hong Kong. For material and outline on the concept of Chinese healing I am grateful to Dr. S. T. Hsiao, surgeon, Kiangsu Divisional Hospital and Dr. S. C. Hsiao, herbalist, Central Hospital of Chinese Medicine, Chiangso Province, China.

For generous support and help on breathing control and Chinese martial arts, I am grateful to William K. W. Hu, a very qualified martial artist with fifteen years of serious dedicated training. For her experiences as a Ch'i Kung practitioner, I thank Christine Sueda, graduate, student at the University of Hawaii. The arrows showing the movements were drawn by Edgar Ng, a very talented artist who sacrificed much of his time in order to do a better job.

Instructions for the sitting forms were written by Walter Y. S. Pang, a recent graduate of the University of Hawaii and a young man with much internal beauty. Instructions for the standing forms were written by Francis Pang, another graduate student at the University of Hawaii.

For the photographs, I am grateful to Delwin Ching, Dai Yen Loo, Calvin Chee and William Hee Jr.

For a great amount of time spent in editing, I am indeed grateful to Kevin Wakayama, of Columbia University.

Mrs. Arlene Luster deserve special thanks for the great amount of paper work and bibliographic searches she so generously did.

Many others have spent much time supporting this work. These people include Raymond Young, Thomas Zane, Dr. C. W. Hsu and many others.

Most importantly, I would like to thank my master, S. F. Chang for the ten years of training he has given me, his encouragement and continued guidance in the theoretical and practical aspects of Ch'i Kung. He told me always:

Ch'Ih te K'u chung K'u
Fang wei jen shang jen

> One who can taste the bitterest of bitterness
> is one who can be a man above men.

Lily Siou

THE PA KUA

Everything under the sun is supposed to originate from the Yin (陰) and the Yang (陽). These two elements are diagramatically represented by a circle called the great absolute or infinite void (八卦) and which is divided into two pear-shaped bodies by a   double curved line. Surrounding these elements are eight trigrams, the Pa Kua (太極) which are made up of a combination of triple lines — whole and broken — arranged in such a manner as not to repeat the combination. This Pa Kua is supposed to have been revealed to Fu Hsi on the back of a supernatural animal called a dragon-horse, that rose from the waters of the Yellow River.

The Pa Kua in Pairs of Opposite Qualities

Each of the eight trigams has a special name with a symbolic and fanciful meaning. But no one has been able to give a definite interpretation of them. Confucius was greatly enamoured of these figures and said that if he could devote fifty years to the study of these lines, he might attain wisdom.

Opposite page: A special work dedicated to Shih Yü, or "Lady Scholar" (a nickname for Lily Siou) by the famed scholar Tseng Ke-tuan. Written in the Seal-Style, Clerical-Style, Real-Style, and the Cursive-Style, each shows the names of the eight trigrams.

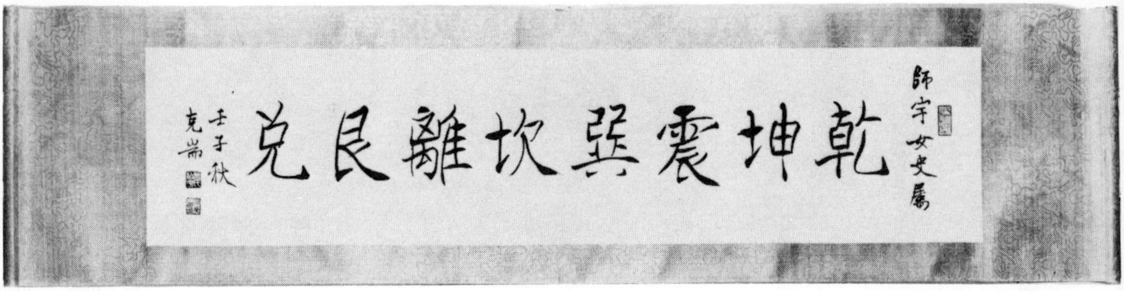

師宇女史屬
壬子秋
克端
兌艮離坎巽震坤乾

師宇女史屬
壬子秋
克端
兌民籲坎華震坤乾

師宇女史屬
壬子秋初
克端
兌艮離坎巽震坤乾

師宇女史屬
壬子秋
克端
兌艮離坎巽震坤乾

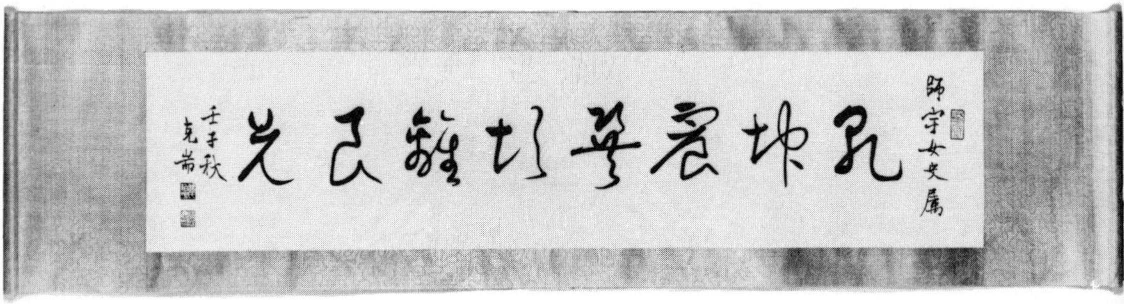

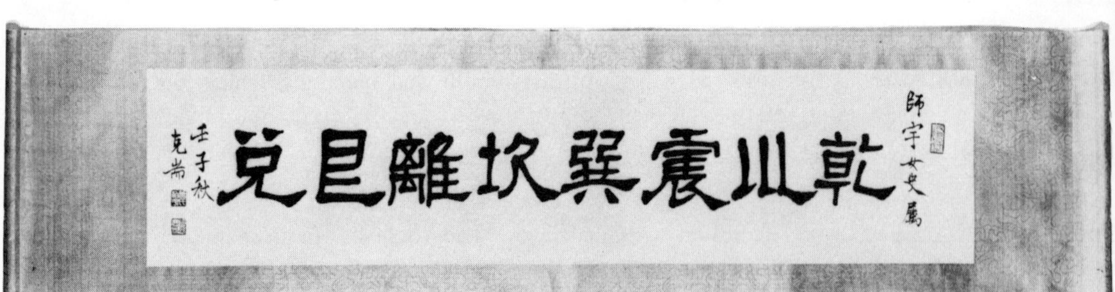

Ch'i Kung: The art of mastering the unseen life force

Table of contents

PART I

THE STANDING FORMS
Salutation (not included in this book)

一日不可閒

八卦是良因誠克崇

造化合乾坤循環次第轉身子

笑病不能侵子後午前作

夢寐不侵驚寒暑不相入

暗想遍燒身氣時口中生津液

體想遍燒大火及近身

火遍燒大遍焚及搬運

託攏肩搬運汨汨

響百三十三度興神也如口

分三十三漉漉再漱再嚥各如

此三漉三漱古今取生津再嚥

分如久嚥水二鈎次頂頭

每用意送十數次頂頭

用舌攪水上次形

生心或按頭

生候心舌低後頭

頻心或以按手兩舉

三下以手托脚鼻舟等法

次手之放入想肩手攀手托或向直少關

之放入次少肩眼轉田氣之精搖運

想肩手鞭身以運精搖運是

手攀身炊鑪出腦大雙又鑪田氣之精是

燒身雨鼻火運門徐將手

将將鼻款少

以外掌王氣根

摩熱

一燒臍口掌腎摩研

輪氣心之後熱研

口開以再摩中精晤之

PART I

八段錦口訣

垂目冥心坐，握固靜思神。

叩齒三十六，兩手抱崑崙。

左右鳴天鼓，二十四度聞。

微擺撼天柱，赤龍攪水津。

漱津三十六，神水滿口勻。

一口分三咽，龍行虎自奔。

PART

THE CONCEPT OF BREATHING CONTROL

"In the beginning to learn the proper use of breath, one should inhale a breath through the nose. Stop up the nose and mentally count one's heart beats. The breath should be exhaled through the mouth. In this method of breathing, everyone should make it his aim that his own ears might not hear the sound of either inhalation or exhalation. The rule is to inhale generously and exhale sparingly. One should suspend the feather of a wild goose in front of the nose and mouth that the feather might not stir while the breath is being expelled should be one's aim. With gradual practice, One should increase correspondingly the count of the heart beats during which the breath is held. After a very long period of time, one should be able to count a thousand heart beats. When an old man has arrived at that stage, then he will be transformed into a young man. . . each day adding to the transformation." – Pao Po Tzu.

Dr. Ko Hung, 470 B.C.

Chapter 1: Body energy or the unseen life force

Everything created by the Tao is part of the unseen life force, and Tao is the creative and receptive principle in the universe. In the universe, there exists two primal forces — the negative and the positive, light and darkness — which make up the Great Whole or the Tao. These two forces exist in that which is microcosmic to that which is macrocosmic.

Energy flows from left to right and right to left unceasingly and is evidenced in changes. It flows like the flowing of a mountain stream. The Chinese consider blood circulation akin to a flowing steam. Only natural flowing water like a river can bring forth life and growth. The Chinese call flowing water, "alive," as water in a swimming pool, which does not flow is "dead." Nothing can be grown, and if the water is not changed, it will soon decay and bad elements like mosquitoes will be created.

The Chinese understood the Tao, or Nature, from which all beings are conceived. They understood that all life is embodied with an unseen life force — a force which can be cultivated and developed to enable one to live life more fully. Ch'i Kung seeks to nurture the unseen life force.

Our prehistoric ancestors, residing in the cave and the forest, lived in harmony with Nature. They watched the trees grow, and saw the animals at play. They watched the seasons pass, and listened to the flowing of mountain streams. By living in Nature, they understood the life-giving force of Nature. The life force was the source of all existence.

To our ancestors, life was a cycle of changes, coming and going like the four seasons. This understanding is recorded in one of the world's oldest books, the I CHING, OR THE BOOK OF ETERNAL CYCLES OF CHANGES:

> *"The Great Attribute, the Moral Character, or the Power of*
> *Heaven produces and reproduces the changes in the universe.*

Changes represent the unseen movement of the creative and the receptive forces. Because of the movement of the creative and the receptive forces, all things come into existence, change, and pass on into other forms. The inter-relationship of the two forces bring transformation of all things — a transformation which proceeds to fullness."

The art of Ch'i Kung is based on the Tao, or the Way of Nature. The first eight forms of Ch'i Kung, called the Eight Silken Forms, show this affinity with Tao. They give one the feeling of peace and tranquility, and of harmony with Tao.

The forms, and sequences of forms in Ch'i Kung open and close the doors between the creative and receptive forces. All things are created, changed and transformed by the movement of force through the doors. Closing the doors, between creative and receptive stops movement. Like stagnant water, stagnant force leads to decay. Opening the door leads to circulation of force and creation. By opening and closing the doors quickly, the unseen life force moves first one way and then the other way. This rapid circulation of force is called active involvement.

Change is caused by the process of opening and closing the door between the primal forces. The creative and receptive forces are virile and docile, respectively. One gives force while the other receives force. The creative force is the light element, which when dormant, is absorbed, and when active, moves forward and creates. The receptive force is the dark element, which when shut by the door, is dormant and inactive, and when opened, receives from the creative force and creates.

The process of opening and closing is the key to regulating the unseen life force. One can control (have access to) inner strength and outward power. The art of Ch'i Kung teaches one the process of opening and closing.

One is born with the unseen life force, and it is this which gives us life. By understanding what it is, and by being able to control it, one is able to enrich one's life. Life becomes harmonious; because one lives closer to the Tao, or the Way of Nature.

Chapter 2: Chinese concept of ch'i and kung

By understanding what "the unseen life force" is, we can readily grasp the concept of "Ch'i." In Chinese, Ch'i means the flowing of the unseen life force. Because of the differences between Western and Eastern culture, there can be no exact translation of the Chinese character, Ch'i (氣). In Chinese, the character for Ch'i symbolizes the original mentality and vitality of the individual. These two sources conjoin to create a nurturing energy which is best defined in English as the internal body energy or the unseen life force.

In Chinese biological terms, Ch'i is the main influence in bringing greater physiological vitality and psychological stability.

In Chinese, "Ch'i" literally menas: breath, health, steam, air, and weather. The character for Ch'i is often seen on Taoist "good luck" charms to bring good health or hygiene.

The character, Ch'i, is widely used in combination with other characters to form new words. "Ch'i Fa" means vaporization or successive changes. "Ch'i Hou" is a solar term meaning weather or climate. In ancient China, an "hou" (候) was a five day unit. Three "hous" constituted a "chiai", and a "chiai ch'i" (節氣) was one of the 24 calendar divisions in a year.

In Chinese philosophy, the "Er ch'i" (二氣) means the dual powers of the Yin and the Yang. The literal meaning of "Er ch'i" is "double original force."

Most of the Chinese martial arts depend on the cultivation of the Ch'i, or body energy. By doing so, one is in harmony with the universe. One is more powerful and more aware. "Liang ch'i" (鍊氣) is one of the Taoist breathing control exercises that help to develop the Ch'i.

Ch'i also means manner, demeanor, constitution, temper, or life-giving force. "Li ch'i" means strength, power, or vigorous constitution. "Yuan ch'i" means inherited constitution.

9

In Chinese religion, Ch'i is the soul or the spirit. If the Ch'i leaves the body, then man would be just a body without life or the will to live. Ch'i is the source which nourishes the existence of life. Man is born with Ch'i, or the unseen life force. Without Ch'i, man is an empty body. The Taoists believe that man is made up of three "Ch'is: (1) the principle of constitution, (2) the original constitution, (3) the true spirit of constitution.

Ch'i has great significance in every field of human endeavor. A writer is said to need "Wen ch'i" or a literary or scholarly disposition. A calligrapher needs a special characteristic or style of brush control called "pi chi." A hero needs heroic style or heroic comportment called "Ch'i Tzu." A professional speaker needs a charismatic and expressive style of speech called "Yu Ch'i." And the average person needs proper understanding of his natural capacity to deal with people called "Ch'i Liang."

In this book, Ch'i means the flowing of the unseen life force. In instances where Ch'i means something else, the usage of the term will be explained.

The Chinese character Kung symbolizes physical power and the mainfestation of this power in the natural movements of the body. The unity or natural integration of physical power and movement is the technique and power of Art. This Art is the means to nurturing the Ch'i or the flowing of the unseen life force. And this is called Kung.

In Chinese literature, Kung means: merit, achievement, efficacy, and good results. "Kung Hsi" (功行) means successful undertaking, or a great stock of merit and ability. In everyday language, Kung means action. "Kung Yung" (功用) means power in action or the beneficial result of an operation or function. When "Kung" is used for right action, it has beneficial results. When an acupuncturist uses one small needle to cure a big illness, we say that the operation was "Kung Yu" (功有) or a divine efficacy.

In this book, Kung means the power of action and movement. This is like the movement of the Ch'i Kung sequence.

Ch'i and Kung have been explained separately to give a fuller understanding of what these terms mean. The two characters are applied in many different ways with different meanings.

Ch'i signifies the flowing of internal energy which is manifested in the sequence shown in the pictures. The flowing sequences suggest how the internal energy should be flowing inside.

Kung signifies the external power of Art. This is shown by the hand, body, and feet movements in the pictures.

Through the practice of Ch'i Kung, one gains the Art of internal and external power and strength.

With this knowledge of internal force and external power, we can apply ourselves more efficiently in our daily living. Our ancestors learned to use trees for building houses and other things. In the same way, man can learn to use the unseen life force to live a more fulfilling life.

Chapter 3: Theory and Philosophy behind the art of chʹi kung

China is one of the oldest nations in the world. She is the cradle of a very ancient civilization; older, perhaps, than the civilizations that grew up in Egype, Babylonia, and Assyria; and also, these ancient cultures passed away long before the birth of Christ while China continues to grow and flourish.

It is not known who the first Chinese were, or where they came from. They were not the original inhabitants of the area which became China. Some believe that the Chinese originated in the rich basin of the Euphrates, the mother of all races. They migrated eastward to the Shansi province in the Yellow River Valley around the 23rd century, B.C. Like the Chaldeans and the Israelites, they were a pastoral people. But after the Chinese had wrested possession of the land from the aboriginal tribes, they became an agricultural people.

The legendary Emperor Shen Nung was believed to be the founder of agriculture. "Shen" means spirit or god, and "Nung" means agriculture. Shen Nung was revered as the patron god of agriculture. He is associated with the Way of Nature as farming is a livelihood that depends on harmony with nature. He showed the Chinese that one must break ground, plant, cultivate, and harvest in accord with the natural passing of seasons.

The early history of China abounds in myths and legends. By these tales, man was able to explain things he didn't understand. But as time passed, experiences gave him empirical knowledge. Many old arts were developed by our ancestors through trial and error and the passing of many centuries. Ch'i Kung, the art of breathing control, is one of the oldest arts in China and it was developed in this way. It began long before written hisotry, and reached its golden age of development during the Chou Dynasty, 1122-255 B.C. Each succeeding dynasty, up to the communist takeover, sustained and practiced this art.

According to the old tales, everything began from Chaos, or the Great Void. Within

Chaos, there existed the three primary elements of the universe — form, force, and substance. But they were still undivided and existed as one. The early tales of cosmology explain that force was first to separate from the Great Void. It was followed by form then substance. The last stage, when substance appears, is called the Great Homogeneity. The universe was complete, but there was no distinction between heaven and earth. Then the lighter and purer substances rose up and created the heavens, and the coarser and heavier substances sank and produced the earth. The division of substance into lighter and heavier parts manifest the Chinese belief in dual power. The Way of Nature is accomplished by the interaction of dual power, and not by the will of a single power such as the Christian God.

The sequences of Ch'i Kung were formulated according to the concept of dual power. Action, or movement, is made up of a gentle part and a forceful part. One may move slowly and gracefully, or one may move quickly and forcefully. Ch'i Kung brings the dual power of movement into harmony. As an example, one begins Ch'i Kung practice with the gentle movements of the Yin and progresses to the forceful movements of the Yang. Each part is essential to each other, and each must be practiced at the right time in order to maintain harmony.

According to legend, 500,000 years passed between the beginning of the world and the ascension of the Emperor Fu Hsi, the founder of the Chinese Nation. During that period, there were countless traditional stories describing the origin of customs, arts and industries. There are no facts of this period, just stories. Anthropologists tell us that primitive peoples all over the world have basically the same customs and beliefs. It is only through the passage of time that human cultures have become distinct and individual. Each culture gradually evolved from a lower and simpler form of life to a higher and more complex one.

The art of Ch'i Kung developed in a similar manner. At first, the theory and practice was simple, but the art progressed to more complex and more refined stages. This progression is naturally reflected in the practice of Ch'i Kung, where one starts with the simple and then goes to the complex.

Before animal husbandry and agriculture, the primitive Chinese lived in caves and survived by anything that came their way. They ate wild fruit, drank the blood of animals, and covered their loins with skins. They had to fight wild beasts and often were hurt of wounded. This is another reason for the development of Ch'i Kung. The cave dwellers needed to be in control of their body energy in order to survive.

Ch'i Kung also aided them in preventing illness and speeding recovery. Meals were irregular and the food coarse and uncooked. The body was exposed to the weather and subject to much abuse. Stomach trouble and other ailments naturally followed. Through experience, they learned methods to fight illness. For example, when they were ill, they lay still in caves and waited for death. After long experience, they discovered that by not moving or exercising, their bodies decayed and they died. By practicing certain exercises, they learned that the sick could become well again. They also found that exercises helped to maintain good health. These exercises were developed over thousands of years and came to be known as Ch'i Kung.

These exercises were developed naturally from instinctive responses to illnesses. The most universal symptom of disorder in the living organism is pain. The organism instinctively seeks to find remedies for it. For example, the dog licks its wounds, and eats certain herbs and grasses when sick. A child will naturally stretch its cramped limbs or scratch its itching body to remove these irritations. Such instinctive responses are the origins from which definite curative systems have arisen.

Primitive man had a very limited knowledge of physical laws or cause and effect. He was in the very first stages of understanding the workings of Nature. The only way for him to explain things was to personify them. He attributed to all inanimate objects his own sentiments and passions, fancying them to be influenced by the same things in the same ways. This tendency to personify or animate everything is universal among primitive peoples.

Primitive man considered natural phenomena to be alive and to have human characteristics. He was frightened by lightning, thunder, earthquakes, volcanic eruptions, and eclipses. He was in awe of the sun, the moon, and the stars. To him all things were the outward manifestations of the gods, demons, and other powerful forces of the universe.

Primitive man thought that health and disease were controlled by these forces. Disease, in particular, was regarded as the work of devils or spirits in possession of the body. The possessed could only be cured of infirmity when the intruders were evicted by the application of appropriate incantations. Charms and other psycho-spiritual practices were used as well as martial exercises for health. In the early stages of Ch'i Kung development, the art was once a faith-and-nature healer as well as a martial art.

Chapter 4: Ch'i kung and the yin and yang

The Yin and Yang are the source of all things in the universe. It is the motherhood and the fatherhood of creation. Heaven was created by an accumulation of Yang, and earth was created by an accumulation of Yin.

The way of Yin and Yang is the way of the left and the right. The Ch'i Kung forms and sequences were born from this concept of the Way.

There are eight feature symbols in the art of Ch'i Kung. The first two are the creative heaven and the receptive earth. They represent the primary division of Yin and Yang in the Ch'i Kung exercises. Under these two, come the elements of fire and water, thunder and wind, and mountain and lake. Each pair is composed of opposites in quality that balance each other. One element is Yin while the other is Yang. Water, wind, and lake are Yin, and fire thunder, and mountain are Yang. Water seeks the lowest ground, while fire seeks to rise into the air. Because fire ascends into heaven and water descends to earth, we can see that Heaven is the accumulation of Yang and earth the accumulation of Yin.

Yin and Yang are also rest and motion controlled by the Way of Nature or the Tao. Fire naturally rises and water naturally seeks the stillness of the low ground. By the movement of Yin and Yang, Nature creates and nourishes life. Ch'I Kung follows the Way of Nature and controls the movement of Yin and Yang. One learns to create, to nourish, and to harvest the unseen life force.

Ch'i Kung exercises harness the flowing of the Yin and the Yang. Through the Yin and the Yang, the transformations of the universe come about. Power and strength are brought forth by Ch'i Kung. It is the beginning of creation within the human body.

Everything in creation is covered by heaven and supported by earth. That which is not created yet is covered by the Yin which in this sense becomes the ruler of the Yang.

15

Chinese cosmology explains that there are many forms of the dual power. The shady side of the hill is Yin, while the sunny side of the hill is Yang. Yin corresponds to the shady, cloudy element, while Yang stands for the sunny and clear element. Yang tends to expand and to flow upward and outward. Yin tends to contract and flow downward. Yang is like the sun, the creative and nourishing source. Yin is like the moon. Yang ascends to heaven and Yin descends to earth. Ascending and descending follow the laws of form, force, and substance. Thus, the law of Yin and Yang bring forth through transformations. From there one gains strength and power through the practice of Ch'i Kung. The law of Yin and Yang follows the harmony of the Tao. The Tao is the key to the mysterious intermingling of heaven and earth. Tao guides us in the way of this world and the beyond by shaping earthly conduct to correspond completely with the demands of the other world.

From the beginning the Chinese viewed everything according to this law. Over thousands of years, they have built up a unique understanding of the relationship between man and the universe.

Chinese philosophy states that the human body is divided into three sections of Yang. Knowing which part was Yin and which part was Yang was important for diagnosis and treatment. The Yin contains:

> the great Yin or Tai Yin
> the small Yin or Hsiao Yin
> the pure Yin or Chia Yin
> the great Yang or Tai Yang
> the small Yang or Hsiao Yang
> the pure Yang or Chia Yang.

In Chinese physiology, each Yin organ is related to a Yang organ. In general, the different sections are related in the following way: the great Yin to the pure Yang, the small Yin to the great Yang, and the pure Yin to the small Yang.

The liver belongs to the pure Yin and thus is related to the gall bladder which belongs to the small Yang. The heart belongs to the small Yin and is related to the small intestines of the great Yang. The spleen belongs to the great Yin and is related to the stomach which belongs to the pure Yang.

In Chinese physiology, the interior of the body is Yin and the exterior is Yang. One must remember that everything is both Yin and Yang, and that the interior of the body is Yin because it is mostly so. Yin is active on the inside and is the guardian of Yang. Yang is active on the outside and is the regulator of Yin.

The relationship of Yin and Yang within the human body has a great influence on one's heath. Perfect harmony between the two primal forces brings good health. The practice of

Ch'i Kung is aimed at achieving this perfect harmony.

All Chinese medical practices can be summed up under one law, which is the Tao and the interplay of Yin and Yang. Through Ch'i Kung, one may gain an understanding of these concepts. Through practice, the wise will finally realize the Tao or the Way of Nature. The ancient Chinese sages understood this and practiced their philosophy and knowledge of Tao in order to attain the harmony between heaven and earth.

It is difficult to express clearly the Chinese philosophy of Tao. It is unfortunate that this book cannot be more detailed and thus gives the readers and students a better understanding of it.

Through the practice of Ch'i Kung, one finds the ability to create and develop his vital energy. The energy of Yin and Yang flows from right to left and left to right. This means that where there is Yin, there is Yang and where there is Yang there is Yin. And Yin and Yang are everywhere. This flowing of the life force or vital energy is called Ch'i.

It is extremely important that the student understands the concept of Yin and Yang. He must have this knowledge before he can make progress in the practice and application of Ch'i Kung. Like the eternal Tao, harmony in the art of Ch'i Kung is reached only when theory and practice complement one another.

Even the younger Chinese generation has difficulty understanding their own philosophy of Yin and Yang. There is a great need for more masters to teach Ch'i Kung. It would be a pity to lose this ancient Chinese wisdom and practice that have developed over the thousands of years.

Understanding of the Tao and the 12 propositions is a prerequisite for the study and practice of Ch'i Kung and other related Chinese martial arts. There is no door or mystery which can remain locked or unsolved when one stresses the study of the Yin and the Yang.

In order to understand the creation of the universe, one must ask what was the agent of creation rather than who. In ancient times, the sages of the Far East realized that anthropomorphic explanations hindered the attainment of enlightenment and wisdom. The Chinese explanation of creation is based on the Tao, or the Way of Nature. This concept is first found in the TAO TE CHING which is attributed to the great philosopher, Lao Tzu. He explains the creation in this manner:

> The Tao gives birth to one.
> And one gives rise to two.
> Two becomes three.
> In this manner, the universe was created.

All things in the universe cannot deny their creation from the Tao and the Yin and the Yang. All things depend on the Tao and the harmony of Yin and Yang.

Life is like the universe in that there is organization and disorganization. Where there is life, there is death, and where there is death, there is life. The Yin and the Yang cannot exist without each other. Where there is one, there is the other. Because of this, life and the Way of Nature encompasses all things. Like the passing of seasons, life includes both summer and winter. Life is like the passing of seasons; there is always movement and change.

Chapter 5: Chinese concept of healing

The previous chapters have explained the basic concepts of Yin and Yang. An understanding of the Yin and Yang is necessary for comprehending the Chinese concept of healing. Many of the principles and practices in Chinese medicine are derived from the philosophy of the Tao.

The natural order of the universe is the Tao. The sun rises and sets at its appointed hour because that is the natural order of the Tao. The moon follows the way of Tao as it goes through its human phases. The seasons come and go according to the Tao.

Tao is the law of heaven and the law of earth. All things, whether they are constant or changing, are following the Tao. Everything obeys the Tao because it is the righteousness of the universe and the harmony of Yin and Yang. Under the Tao, all things follow a definite order.

The Chinese believe that illness is caused by disharmony within the body. When the forces of the body stray from the Tao, or the natural order, the body cannot function properly. The forces of Yin and Yang must be in harmony for good health.

The Chinese physicians treat their patients by correcting the harmony of Yin and Yang. They examine the organ which is in disorder. If the organ has a deficiency of Yang, the doctor must stimulate the Yang. If the Yang was in excess, the doctor would have to calm it down in order to achieve balance. The concepts of Chinese philosophy are important for treating disease and illness.

The Chinese medical practices of acupuncture and cauterization follow very closely the philosphy of Tao. The Chinese classified the body into fourteen meridians, with each meridian consisting of many points. Each point referred to a different organ. By inserting needles, different organs or body functions could be stimulated or repressed. Acupuncture has an excellent record of achieving positive results.

In this book, acupuncture and cauterization will be explained briefly as the authoress has written a book on these practiced. Interested readers may refer to it for a more complete explanation.

The practice of acupuncture started in the Stone Age. Anthropologists have discovered stone needles dating back before the Chinese Bronze Age. In the ancient Chinese classic, "Sun Hsi Ching," there is a reference to acupuncture:

> *In the range of the Eastern Sea,*
> *There are stones that look like jade,*
> *They glisten, and brighten the four quarters,*
> *They can be made into needles*
> *To cure a hundred illnesses.*

According to the folk legends, the Yellow Emperor invented the art of acupuncture. According to historical records, the celebrated physician, Pien Ch'iao, was the greatest master of acupuncture techniques.

In the Tang Dynasty, acupuncture was one of the seven branches of medicine. A special chair was established at the medical university for the professor in charge of this art. During the Sung Dynasty, acupuncture was elevated to a science. The first monographs of acupuncture were published during this period.

In 1027 A.D., the reigning emperor of the Sung cast two copper models of the human body for the teaching of this science. The models were marked with the 365 acupuncture points that were known then. It was thought that there was a magical symmetry between the number of points and the number of days in a year. Each point had its own name and a specific relationship with the internal organs.

The acupuncture operation, in its basic form, consists of inserting needles of varying shapes and sizes into certain points of the body. There are nine distinct categories of needles: arrow-headed, blunt, puncturing, spearpoint, ensiform, round, capillary, long, and great. The first needles were made of stone, bamboo, and bone. Later needles were made of copper, steel, gold, and silver.

The needles are inserted into the flesh to a depth varying from 1/10 of an inch to 4½ inches. During insertion, the patient is usually ordered to cough, in order to distract his attention and to relax his muscles. The needles may be inserted by hand or by a blow from a light mallet. The needles may be hot or cold depending on the type of ailment. Occasionally, the needles are left in the site for a number of days. The point of insertion, the direction of the needles' rotation, the number of needles, the depth of the puncture, and the length of time they are left in, all depend upon the nature and severity of the case.

Today acupuncture is widely practiced in Europe as well as in Asia. In many places, it is considered a universal panacea. It is used chiefly to cure or alleviate cholera, colic, cough, rheumatism, arthritis, sprains, swollen joints, diseases of the nerves, and internal pains of all kinds.

Chapter 6: Great herbal

The Pen T'sao, (本草) or Chinese Material Medication, is a collection of medical knowledge and practices, stemming from the earliest Chinese. It is thought to be about as old as the art of acupuncture. Scholars believe that from the time of Emperor Shen Nung (2838 B.C.) to the time of the great herbist, Li Shih Chen (李時珍) (1578 A.D.), at least thirty-nine kinds of Pen T'sao have appeared.

The Pen T'sao Ching (本草經) or the Classic of Materia Medication, is believed to be the first compilation of herbal medicine. Tradition ascribes authorship to Shen Nung, a legendary emperor who reigned from 2838 – 2698 B.C. The work consists of three volumes: classifying 365 kinds of drugs into three categories: superior, medium, and inferior. The categories are based on drug potency. This work was not written down until the time of the Han Dynasty. It had been preserved by word-of-mouth over many generations till then.

Since the invention of printing, the Chinese culture was able to record and preserve many books of herbal medicine. The following is a list of some of the herbal classics with a brief description of each.

1. THE TS'AI YAO LU (采藥錄), or The Record of Herb Hunting by T'ung Chun. (桐君)
2. MING I PIEH LU (名醫別錄), or the Special Record of Medicine by Famous Physicians by Tao Hung-Chin.
    He submitted this work to Emperor Wu Ti whose imperial sanction made it China's first official pharmacopoeia.
3. LEI KUNG YAO TUI (雷公藥對) by Hsu Chih Tsai
4. LI SHI YAO LU (李氏藥錄), or the Notes of Medicine by Li Tang-Chih. (李當之)
5. WU SHIH PEN TS'AO (吳氏本草), or the Materia Medicine by Wu P'u.

6. LEI KUNG P'AO (雷公炮炙論) by Lei Hsiao, a disciple of Hua T'o, the great surgeon.

7. T'ANG PEN T'SAO (唐本草).
This is such an important book that Emperor Kao Tsung (625 A.D.) appointed a committee of twenty-two to revise Tao Hung Ching's edition.

8. THE SHU PEN TS'AO (蜀本草), or the Materia Medication of Szechuan by Han Pao-Sheng. (韓保升)

9. K'AI PAO PEN T'SAO (開寶本草), or the Revelation of the Golden Herbal. This book was sanctioned by Emperor Tai Tsu in 973 A.D.

10. CHI YU PU CHU PEN T'SAO (嘉祐補註本草), A Book Of Medical Illustrations gathered from many provinces by the Imperial decree and edited by Su Seng. (蘇頌)

11. CHENG LEI PEN TS'AO (證類本草), or Experiements in Materia Medication. The book was presented to Emperor Hui Tsang by Tang Shen Lei in 1108 A.D.

12. The following books on herbal medicine were written during the Chin and Yuan Dynasties:
   a) Chang Yuan-Su's CHEN CHU NANG (珍珠囊)
   b) Li Kao's YUNG YAO FA HSIANG (用藥法象)
   c) Wang Hao-ku's T'ANG YEH PEN T'SAO (湯液本草)
   d) Wu Jui's JIH YUNG PEN T'SAO (日用本草)
   e) Hu Shih-ko's PEN T'SAO KO KUO (本草歌括)
   f) Chu Chen-hen's PEN T'SAO YEN I PU I (本草衍義補遺)

13. The following books on herbal medicine were written during Ming Dynasty, 1368-1644, the most glorious age for Chinese herbal medicine.
   a) PEN T'SAO FA HUI (本草發揮)
   b) CHIU FANG PEN T'SAO (救荒本草)
   c) KENG HSIN YU T'SE (庚辛玉冊)
   d) SHIH CHIEN PEN T'SAO (食鑑本草)
   e) PEN T'SAO HUI PIENG (本草會編)
   f) PEN T'SAO MENG CH'UANG) (本草蒙荃)
   g) PEN T'SAO PI YAO (本草備要)
   h) SHIH WU PEN T'SAO (食物本草)

14. PEN T'SAO KANG MU (本草綱目), or the Great Herbal by Li Shih Chen also was written during the Ming Dynasty. This work is the most famous and important classic of Chinese medicine and is the standard reference text of Materia Medication Li Shih Chen (1518-1593 A.D.) is revered for his spiritual greatness as well as for his

medical writings. The Great Herbal contains much of his compassions for humanity and of his inspiration to help man through medicine. Physicians fall in love with this book and derive much inspiration from it. Physicians will often have a picture of Li Shih Chen in their homes.

Li Shih Chen was a native of Kin Chow. He started to write his book in 1552 A.D. and finished it in 1578 A.D. In all, he spent twenty-seven years composing this book. Over the next fifteen years, the entire manuscript was revised three times before it reached its final form. Li Shih Chen died shortly after completing the book. His son, Li Chien-Yuan (李建元), submitted the manuscript to the emperor, and the book was published in 1595 A.D.

THE GREAT HERBAL consists of fifty-two volumes. All preceding books on Materia Medication, which number thirty-nine, were consulted. Li Shih Chen also used 360 other medical treaties and 591 other scientific and historical works. The material is arranged in 62 orders under 16 classes: water, fire, earth, metal and mineral, herbs, grains, vegetables, fruits, trees, insects, fish, mollusks, birds, beasts, men, medical garments, and instruments. Li Shih-Chen added 374 new drugs bringing the total number of drugs to 1871. Of the drugs enumerated, 1074 are derived from plants, 443 from animals, and 354 from minerals and other substances. The book contains 142 illustrations and 8160 drug recipes, ancient and modern, selected from previous writings.

The drugs are organized under the proper name of each drug. Its popular names are then listed, with an explanation of their origin and meaning. Next is the information on the drug collected from the medical, scientific, and historical literature. The source, form, and general history of each drug is given. Next are directions for collection, manufacture, dosage, and preservation of the drug. The nature and properties of the drugs, expecially in regards to flavor, smell, color and other characteristics are described. At the end of each section is a large selection of recipes selected from different authors. The recipes may have slightly different uses and some recipes list indicators to test the chemical purity of the drug.

The first four volumes of THE GREAT HERBAL deal with the introductory material. They contain the preface, table of contents, illustrations of the various drugs, the elements of drug dispensing, pharmacology, a discussion of drug incompatibilities, and a list of complimentary and contradictory drugs. Then follows an index of diseases with their appropriate remedies, a discussion of drugs in general, a summary of the contents and an appendix.

Chapter 7: History of chinese medicine

The Chinese culture developed many legends concerning the beginnings of medicine. These legends explain that medicine began with the founders of the Chinese nation. The first founder was Shen Nung, a legendary emperor, who was supposed to have reigned from 2898-2698 B.C. It is said that he had the head of an ox and was born with great wisdom.

Shen Nung taught the people how to cultivate the five grains for food. The list of five grains vary, depending on the part of the country. Hemp or flax, two kinds of millet, wheat, barley, pulse, and rice are the grains included in the lists. Shen Nung is worshipped even today by the native agriculture guilds as their patron god. On the first and fifteenth day of every month, incense and offerings are put before his shrine. On these days many employers treat their employees to a special dinner in honor of Shen Nung. He is considered by all Chinese to be the founder of agriculture.

Shen Nung is honored also as the discovered of the Hundred Herbs and as the first founder of medicine. Also, on the first and fifteenth days of the month, doctors and pharmacists give a 10% discount on all drugs. In most cities, a temple of medicine is erected to perpetuate his memory. As the first founder, he is revered as the "Father of Medicine."

Another legendary character in Chinese medicine was Huang Ti, the Yellow Emperor, who reigned from 2698-2598 B.C. In collaboration with Ch'i Pai (岐伯), one of his talented ministers, he is said to have written the famous classic, NEI CHING, or the Yellow Emperor's Classic of Internal Medicine. The medical profession is sometimes spoken of as the "Art of Ch'i" and "Huang" in honor of the Yellow Emperor and his minister. Historical research, however indicates that the NEI CHING was written much later, around the end of the Chou Dynasty, 1122-255 B.C. Still, this is more than 2000 years ago, making the NEI CHING the oldest book of medicine in the world.

THE SHIH CH'I, or Historical Records of China contain much biographical information on famous physicians. This material is as much legendary as it is factual.

They record that Yu Fu, one of China's greatest surgeons, was able to perform organ transplants in the third century B.C. His greatest achievement was a successful heart transplant in 255 B.C. He was also able to clean out the alimentary tract by operating on the stomach and washing out the intestines.

Yu Fu and later surgeons were resisted by the Confucians and Taoists. Both groups considered the body to be sacred. In addition, they felt that surgery was a crude and unnecessary method of healing. By interfering with the unity and integration of the human body, they felt that surgery was harmful in the long run.

Other great surgeons were Pien Chiao of the second century, B.C. and Hua To of the third century, A.D.. Hua To was the last of the great surgeons.

The art of surgery gave way to other medical arts, primarily acupuncture, herbal medicine, cauterization, and Ch'i Kung.

The first Chinese doctors were priests. According to legend, Sorcerer Peng, or Wu Peng, was the first priest doctor. At the beginning of Chinese medicine, faith-healing was often employed. The Su Wen, or the first chapter or the NEI CHING, discusses faith healing and old superstitions, medical practices. These primitive methods of treatment consisted of diverting one's thoughts from illness by changing the physical environment and by prayer. These psychological methods were often the only cures that the early Chinese had.

The Su Wen records that the priests of old knew the essential points about the diseases, and that some, like Sorcerer Peng, were quite successful in treatment.

According to the SHU CHING CHIN TENG, or the Book of History, faith healing was resorted to, even by the educated classes. Chou Kung, the Duke of Chou, cured King Wu's illness through prayer. King Wu, a brilliant ruler, was the first king of the Chou Dynasty.

Even in the ANALECTS OF CONFUCIUS, Tzu Hu, a famous disciple of Confucius, records that he offered to pray for Confucius when the master was sick.

In the ancient periods of Chinese history, medical practice was largely a matter of superstition, and psychotherapy as well as herbal medicine.

Although the legends state that Chinese medicine started with Fu Hsi Shen Nung, and Huang Ti, the three legendary emperors, historians do not know when Chinese medicine began. It would be safe to say, however, that wherever there are people, there is a need for medicine. Man instinctively tries to find means to cure his illness. Animals intuitively find remedies for their illnesses. They know what kind of grasses to eat for certain ailments. Dogs lick their wounds without knowing that their saliva combat germs and cures certain skin diseases. With man's great intelligence improvement could not have been far away.

Chapter 8: Two doctrines

The Chou Dynasty, which began in 1122 B.C., was one of the most creative periods in Chinese history. The middle period of Chou, around 700 B.C., was a glorious period where there was great accomplishment in the fields of medicine, literature, painting, philosophy, religion, government, and historical writing. Every part of this civilization flourished.

The "Chou I," or I CHING, was completed at this time. It is the oldest known book on philosophy in the world. For further understanding, refer to the authoress' book "I Ching: The Book of Eternal Cycle of Changes."

The Chou Dynasty is rightly called the Age of Philosophy. Confucius, Mencius, Lao Tzu, Chuang Tzu, Kuan Tzu, Lieh Tzu, Hsun Tzu, and most of the other famous philosophers of China lived in this period. These philosophers, especially Confucius, Mencius, and Lao Tzu, were men of great genius and contributed to every branch of literature, art, and philosophy. Their ideas became deeply ingrained in the Chinese culture.

Medicine before the middle Chou period had fallen into scholastic stagnation. Medicine was no longer an effective, practical art based on observation and empirical and deductive knowledge. Instead, masquerading under the name of medicine, was a pretentious system of healing that was excessively theoretical and almost theatrically elaborate. Like the European alchemists of the Dark Ages, the Chinese physicians of early Chou were complicating the art, abusing the empirical principles, and becoming less and less effective in practice. The study of medicine was dominated by mystical philosphers and was characterized by reverence for authority, petrified formalism, and pedantic excess of detail.

There was much debate on the theory of medical practice during the middle Chou period and the causes of disease. As a result, the scholasticists and pendants were overthrown. The new medical establishment evolved two doctrines which became the foundation of the whole of Chinese medicine. The two doctrines were the doctrine of the Yin and the Yang, and the doctrine of the five elements.

The fundamental principle of the new medicine was empirical evidence and experience over theory and speculation. The nature healing arts of Ch'i Kung, T'ai Ch'i Ch'uan and the soft art of Kung Fu are based on the two doctrines. They are the products of accumulated knowledge on the care of the body, the mind, and the spirit.

The first doctrine is the doctrine of the two principles or the doctrine of the Yin and the Yang. The Yin and the Yang are the two primal forces in the universe. Everything originates from them. They are usually symbolized by a circle called the Great Absolute or the Supreme Ultimate. In Chinese, the circle, which symbolized their unit, is called the T'ai Ch'i.

Everything exists between the Yin and the Yang. For this reason, they are called the two modes of extremity. These two modes gave birth to eight trigrams, or Pa Kua. The eight trigrams are supposed to date from Emperor Fu Hsi, the first emperor of China. The trigrams were revealed to him by a supernatural animal called the dragon horse. This divine creature, which was half Yin and half Yang, was sent to him by the gods with the trigrams printed on its back. The creature is said to have risen from the waters of the Yellow River.

Each of the eight trigrams has a special name with a symbolic and mystical meaning. No one has ever been able to understand the meanings of the trigrams. Even Concucius said that if he could devote fifty years to study the trigrams; there was only the possibility that he might gain their wisdom.

The eight trigrams are partially interpreted by the I CHING. In the casting of fortunes, each trigram is symbolized by three lines. The unbroken lines are called Yang, and the broken lines Yin.

Chien, the Yang or active principle in nature, i.e., heaven the Father. The North West point of the compass, etc.

Tui, lake, gentle, the youngest daughter or a young girl, ascending vapor, lightness, the West.

Li, five, eight, warmth, intelligent, the middle daughter (or middle aged female) on life, etc. The South.

Chen, thunder, the swift power of nature, igneous exhalation or the oldest son (strong man) etc. The East.

Sun, the wind, expansive energy, flexibility or the oldest daughter, etc. The South East.

28

═══   K'an, water, the flowing element. The rigidity, cold, or the middle son,
─ ─   etc. The North.

───   Ken, mountains, the keeping still, solidity, gravity, quiet or the youngest
─ ─   son, etc. The North East.

─ ─   K'un, the earth, the yin or receptive principle in nature, obedient,
─ ─   submissive, soft, gentle empty, Miss or the mother, etc. The South
      West on the compass card.

In general, the Yin and the Yang may be interpreted as the male and the female. Some of the various manifestations of male-female are: heaven-earth, sun-moon, hot-cold, life-death, positive-negative, strong-weak, light-dark, good-bad, and superior-inferior. All show the principle of polarity.

In Chinese medicine, everything is classified under these two principles. The skin, or surface of the body is Yang, and the interior of the body is Yin. The chest is Yang, and the abdomen is Yin. The empty organs Need The Balance of Yang, and the solid organs Need The Balance of Yin. The heart and liver are Yang organs, and the spleen, lungs, and kidneys are Yin organs.

Yin and Yang, however, are always found together. It is only a matter of degree. Thus within the Yang there is something of the Yin and vice versa. For instance, the chest is Yang, but the lungs are Yin. This is a Yin within a Yang. The abdomen is Yin, but the liver is Yang. This is a Yang within a Yin. The chest and heart are both Yang, and this is a Yang within a Yang. The abdomen and spleen are both Yin, and this is a Yin within a Yin.

Diseases are also classified by Yin and Yang. A Yang disease is due to external causes, and a Yin disease to internal causes. In general, Yang diseases are fever, afflictions of the upper body, respiratory disease, diseases of a sudden nature, and afflictions of the back. Yin diseases are chills, afflictions of the lower body, circulatory diseases, diseases of a gradual nature, and afflictions which don't allow the patient to lie on his back.

When the Yang force is excessive, there is fever and when the Yin force is excessive, there are chills. Drugs are classified according to Yin and Yang. Yin drugs are used for Yin diseases and Yang drugs for Yang diseases.

The second doctrine is the doctrine of the five elements. The five elements are the five primary substances from which all other elements are created. They are fire, wood, earth, metal, and water.

The human body is made of a harmonic mixture of these primary substances. The body will remain healthy as long as the substances are in harmony. If there is an imbalance, if one element is in excess, then the body will become weak and illness will follow.

The five elements correspond with the five primary organs. The heart corresponds with fire, the liver with wood, the spleen with earth, the lungs with metal, and the kidneys with water.

The five primary organs correspond with five external organs. They are linked in some way, and a disease of a primary organ will be manifested by its external organ. The heart communicates with the tongue, the liver with the eyes, the spleen with the mouth, the lungs with the nose, and the kidneys with the ears.

The five elements constantly interact with each other in a process of generation and destruction. Each element has the power to generate an element and to destroy an element.

Wood generates fire, fire generates earth, earth generates metal, metal generates water and water generates wood. Wood destroys earth, earth destroys water, water destroys fire, fire destroys metal, metal destroys wood.

Drugs are classified according to the five elements. Each drug, although composed of each of the five elements, has a primary disposition to one element. A drug with a primary disposition to fire is called a fire drug. It can be used to generate more of the earth element in the body, or to destroy an excess of the metal element.

Another medical art following the Two Doctrines is pulse reading. According to the NEI CHING, or the Yellow Emperor's Book of Internal Medicine, pulse reading consists of four types of diagnosis. They are observation, auscultation, interrogration, and palpitation. The art of pulse reading is the basic method of diagnosis that every Chinese physician learns.

The exact date of the origin of pulse reading is unknown. The first exponent of this art was Pien Chia who lived around 250 B.C. The first book on pulse reading was the MO CHING or The Cannon of the Pulse, by Wang Shu-Ho (circa 280 A.D.) of the Chin Dynasty, 255-206 B.C. The MO CHING is a work of ten volumes that describes all aspects of pulse reading and of diagnosis.

The art of pulse reading is very complicated. The procedure is very detailed and much experience is necessary before a physician becomes proficient.

The physician examines the patient's pulse from both right and left wrists. In most cases, the physician takes the patient's left wrist in his right hand, and the right wrist in his left hand. The physician centers the middle finger on the head of the radius and places the index and ring fingers next to the middle finger. The thumb rests on the dorsum of the carpals:

The physician's metabolism must be in a tranquil state in order to feel the metabolism of the patient. He must be aware of his own breathing and his own pulse rate. The physician usually sets up his metabolism by taking one breath for every four heart beats. After this is done, the physician examines the patient by the four methods of diagnosis. The diagnosis will reveal the location of the disease and the type of disorder.

In China, a number of arts which maintained the health were practiced. These were not medical arts, but rather exercise arts which maintained mental and physical health. As the Chinese proverb says, "No medicine is the best medicine." Foremost among these arts was the art of Breathing Control. In the classic, CHOU LI, six arts were recommended for vitality. They were archery, charioteering, ritual observances, music, writing, and mathematics. Many Chinese philosophers, like the Greeks, recommended breathing control and other forms of recreation for sound bodies, agile minds, and prolonged life. The Taoist, Chuang Tzu said, "By inhalation and exhalation, the foul air was expelled and fresh air taken in, thus producing longevity."

Chapter 9: Five cardinal rules for Chinese doctors

1. Do not delay when called on.
   Treat the poor and the rich in the same manner.
   Give the required attention and medication whether or not the patient can afford to pay.
2. Do not treat a girl, a widow, or a nun unless another person is present. If she has a private disease, examine her carefully and tell no one of the disease, not even your wife.
3. Do not substitute any precious ingredients, such as pearl or amber, entrusted to you in preparing the medicine. It is wiser to advise your patients to compound the medicine themselves in order to avoid suspicion.
4. Do not leave your office during working hours. Do not go to picnics or drinking parties. Attend your patients in person and write your prescriptions clearly and carefully.
5. Do not entertain any impure thoughts when called on to see a prostitute or someone's mistress. Treat them as one from a good family. Leave them as soon as your duty is done. Do not go again unless called on.

Chapter 10: Ch'i kung and the taoists

The art of Ch'i Kung, like many of the other ancient arts, is surrounded by an air of mystery. Even Chinese people do not known much about it. Modern scholars may know the Chinese characters for Ch'i Kung, but few know its meaning. In mainland China today, there is only an handful of qualified teachers and even fewer Ch'i Kung masters.

The Chinese dictionary will define "Ch'i Kung" as "an ancient Taoist breathing exercise." This is incorrect, as Ch'i Kung is an art pre-dating the Taoists. Ch'i Kung is practiced by many groups; however, the Taoists have practiced it the most. A better definition for "Ch'i Kung" would be "an ancient art of breath control based on the early Tao philosophy but predating the Taoists." Ch'i Kung is practiced in its pure form by the Taoists and in its secondary forms of T'ai Ch'i Ch'uan and Kung Fu Boxing by martial artists.

According to legend, Ch'i Kung was practiced at the time of three legendary emperors. The three legendary emperors came before the written history of China. They are mostly cultural stories which enable the Chinese people to have a sense of historical beginning. Only the most ancient practices and arts like Ch'i Kung are said to come from this period of the three emperors. Although the time and place of Ch'i Kung's origin cannot be documented, the legends tell us that Ch'i Kung is an ancient part of China's rich culture.

According to legend, Ch'i Kung was devleoped by a nature loving artist. He was a primitive man who had a great sensitivity towards Nature and developed a sense of beauty. He appreciated the fragrant flowers, bathed in streams of flowing water, and breathed deeply of the fresh, clean air. He cherished the beauty of Nature and grew to appreciate the mysterious and wondrous ways of the universe.

After many years of living in harmony with Nature, he began to learn some of the mysteries of Nature. He found that inhalation supplied him with fresh air and exhalation removed foul air. He also discovered that inhalation and exhalation assisted the circulation of blood. In time, he learned that by controlling his breathing, he could assist the functions of the body. Breathing control could be used for relaxation also to achieve a tranquil state of mind. Physical strength either endurance of sudden power, was enhanced by breathing control. Lastly, this Nature Loving Artist learned that breathing control was the way to longevity.

He also developed beautiful gymnastic forms which complemented the breathing exercises. By coordinating body movements with breathing, breath control became more effective in increasing the vitality of mind and body. The gymnastic forms were combined into beautiful, flowing sequences in order to imitate the beautiful forms and flowing movements found in Nature. This art came to be known as Ch'i Kung. The first eight forms of exercise are called the Eight Silken Forms. The next five forms are called the Playing of the Five Animals — the tiger, the bear, the deer, the monkey, and the bird. From these forms, we can see that the emulation of Nature has played a large part in the development of Ch'i Kung. The last set of thirteen forms is called "The Thirteen Gentle Forms for Self Defense." These forms build up one's health and internal resistance to disease.

The art of Ch'i Kung matured over thousands of years. Variations of the basic Ch'i Kung forms developed into the martial arts of China. During the Chou Dynasty, 1122-255 B.C., one of the most glorious periods of Chinese history, Ch'i Kung was perfected into the art that it is today. It was practiced widely and was respected for its life-giving properties.

The Taoist philosophers believed that Ch'i Kung brought harmony with Nature. The following words of Lao Tzu and Chuang Tzu explain the relationship between Ch'i Kung and the Tao.

> *"Feeding the soul so that it does not die is acquisition of the mysterious celestial breath, and the female terrestral breathing and the openings — through which these mysterious and female breaths enter, are the root and basis of the celestial and terrestrial influences which exist in man. They ought to be inhaled smoothly and slowly, as if they were to be preserved in the body. . . In using those breaths, no exertion is to be made." — Lao Tzu.*

and

> *"Blowing and gasping, sighing and breathing, expelling the old breath and taking in new: Passing time like the dormant bear, and stretching and twisting the neck like a bird. . . All this merely shows the desire for longevity. This is what doctors who inhale, and the men who nourish their bodies, in order to live as long as*

34

Also, Huai Nan Tzu declares that he who consumes the atmosphere becomes spiritual and attains extreme old age.

Lao Tzu, the founder of Taoism, stressed the importance of becoming one with Tao through the harmony of the Yin and the Yang. The techniques of Ch'i Kung were developed according to the philosphy of the Yin and the Yang. The breathing control and gymnastic exercises bring these two forces into harmony. The 152 forms of Ch'i Kung are very close to the Taoist's conception of life.

Lao Tzu's followers, such as Chuang Tzu, practiced Ch'i Kung in order to fulfill his way of life. Chuang Tzu, a famous Taoist philosopher, is noted primarily for the originality and beauty of his writings. He had a keen understanding of the chaos, sufferings, and absurdity that dominated the world of man. Chuang Tzu believed that breathing control gave man strength, vitality, inspiration, and magic powers.

Chang Tao-ling, known as the Taoist pope, was another practitioner of Ch'i Kung, who contributed to the belief that Ch'i Kung was a mysterious art with supernatural qualities. It is said that at the age of seven, he had already mastered the writings of Lao Tzu and the most recondite treatises relating to the philosophy of divination. Devoting himself wholly to study and meditation, he firmly declined the offers of Emperors Ho Ti and Chang Ti. Each tried to bring him into his service of the state by offers of high position and wealth. Chang Tao-ling retired at an early age to the seclusion of the mountains of Western China. He devoted himself to the study of alchemy and the search for an elixer of life. He discovered that Ch'i Kung was a successful means of prolonging life. It is also said that he found a way to immortality by metempsychosis.

Lung Hu Shan, or the Mountain of the Dragon and Tiger in Kiangsi Province, is one of the places where he practiced Ch'i Kung. This mountain has become sacred to his name. Chang Tao-ling lived to 123 years of age and was laid to rest there. He was called the sorcerer of the Ta Tan, or the Grand Elixer. The Ta Tan is another name for Ch'i Kung.

A Taoist School, called Shan Tan, or the Mountain of Elixer, was founded to carry on Chang Tao-ling's teachings. This school, based in Kiangsi Province, is famous throughout China for its practice of Ch'i Kung and the Six Chinese Arts (archery, riding, ritual observances, music, writing, and mathematics). The Shan Tan School is said to have a line of successors from Chang Tao-ling. By metempsychosis, the soul of Chang Tao-ling passes to a newborn infant on his death. The infant then becomes the successor to Chang Tao-ling. His heirship is revealed by certain supernatural characteristics which he possesses. By this means, Chang Tao-ling has achieved immortality. Today, there is a branch of the Shan Tan School in the United States. It was established in Hawaii by its authority through Lily Siou, a 3rd disciple.

Chapter 11: Ch'i kung and the martial arts

A man dressed in loose fitting garments sat by the stream's edge with his flimsy bamboo pole dangling in the crystal clear water hoping that he would catch a fish for his daily supplement. Contented he was, just sitting there and enjoying the confines of nature and relaxing his muscles. He was one with nature, although he knew that tomorrow he may die in his duel with a well known practitioner of a different school. Thus it was, that a practitioner of the martial arts faced life and death with the same indifference. A perfect martial artist knew how to live as well as to die.

Traditionally, Ch'i Kung was an integral part of the martial arts. Witness today, the fierce breathing techniques of the karateka, or the meditative breath control of Chinese martial artists. All this has had its beginnings in the ancient art of Ch'i Kung.

Legendary wise, when one could master the techniques of Ch'i Kung, he could do amazing feats. He would be immune to any type of blows, and was said even to withstand the attack of sword or spear. The Ch'i Kung expert was said to be very strong and that no one could budge him from one spot if he chose to stay rooted to one place. He could also leap as high and as far as twenty feet. He was credited with the power to kill anyone just with a touch of a finger, which the Chinese term as DIM MAK, or death touch. He was said to have been able to avoid attacks because he could actually read or predict the aggressive movements of his adversary. Indeed, it is difficult to believe some of these feats, and if they were accountable for, it would take an immense amount of training to achieve these ends. However, even in today's society, it is possible to develop some powers which would be extraordinary.

The principles of Yin and Yang, and the great and eternal Tao can be applied to the techniques of unarmed combat. For instance, when movements are agressive, and done with much strength, this is a facet of Yang or the male principle. Because the movement is aggressive and seeks to fill a space by its attacks, this indeed the aspect of the male's outward characteristics. Yet, when one blocks using the strength of the attacker, or moves away from a blow, this is in accordance with the Yin or female principle. The Yin principle is empty and mysterious. A passive offense, utilizing little strength is an aspect of the female's unaggressivenes. When one can utilize both of these principles, one has understood the Tao.

To use these principles correctly takes a great deal of experience, intelligence, skill, and patience. When the martial artist has finally mastered these principles, his art has reached the level of perfection. He begins to realize that all unarmed combat must follow these same principles of Yin and Yang regardless of what style one follows. These principles are the foundation of every style. However, this does not mean that every individual who reaches this stage will apply the principles in the same way. Martial artistry is a matter of individual style and differs according to how practitioners interpret and apply the principles to their movements. For example, a practitioner of T'ai Ch'i Ch'uan would look quite different from a fellow practitioner who also learned how to apply the same principles. Another practitioner of a completely different art, such as Karate, would look different in the application of his art to the T'ai Ch'i advocate. Both, however, would have learned the same principles. Indeed, it is hard to pin point any one method as the correct method for the application of all martial arts.

Regardless of what style one chooses to practice, the ultimate comes when he is able to say or feel that his art has become like the Tao. That is, his art would be compared to water or air in that it would be supple and gentle, and that an opponent would not be able to "grasp" his techniques. Speaking of water or air, these elements are intangible and soft, but yet can be harnessed in such a way as to create havoc and destruction everywhere. The martial artist too, must become soft and gentle, and ungraspable, but able to call upon his internal power to defeat any attacker. A blade of grass bends with the wind, but a branch which is brittle and hard succumbs under the power of the wind.

The mind of the martial artist must be open and adapting like the Tao. He must be able to reflect his opponent's moves perfectly without falling to a ruse. He must become one with his opponent and, in so doing, make the opponent fight against himself. The two combatants are merely two parts that make a whole, and the outcome depends on which element is stronger at the time, the Yin or the Yang.

If one were to observe the masters of any martial art, he would soon notice similarities among them. For instance, most of them retain a relaxed and calm manner. Most of their muscles would look soft and supple when not in use. When they enter combat, it becomes a different story; their muscle immediately take on a hardness comparable to steel. It can

37

safely be assumed that their deadly power is indeed hidden and unseen. The martial artist learns to use just the right amount of strength and movement in order to defend himself.

Any great artist knows that in the beginning he must learn the fundamental skills of his art. Similarly, the martial artist who starts out in the beginning, must find a system that fits him. After studying for awhile, he will learn that there is more to the system than meets the eye. In the final stage, when his skill becomes perfected, he discards his system and regains his original freedom, with a difference. The difference is that the system has become ingrained within the man. In other words, the system is demolished, as it becomes the man, and not vice versa. Reaching this final stage is a most difficult task and can be compared to the enlightenment reached by meditation.

In the application of Ch'i Kung to the movements in all martial arts, one must realize that when one assumes a form, all the elements of the Yin and Yang are found there. For instance, when one places most of his weight on one foot and his body is positioned in such a way that most of the body is filling a certain space, we assume that the Yang is the most active in that area of the body, where the Yin is found in the parts of the body where the form is empty or there is no weight to be found there. Likewise, where strength is concentrated up n, the Yang principle is most active here, while the Yin is seen in that area where there is no strength. Generally speaking, the human body is one of the greatest modes of expression for the forms of Yin and Yang. The human body itself, is hard and soft and thus, for this very fact alone, possesses the forms of Yin and Yang. When one assumes a form, we can generally say that this is the Yang principle simply for the fact that the form is tangible and can be rationalized. However, when one begins to change into a different form, we can say that this is the Yin principle which is intangible.

Delving further into the forms of the martial arts and the practice of Ch'i Kung, we find that the sets of forms are really methods of meditation in motion. Ancient practitioners generally seem to agree that this type of meditation is more superior to other forms of meditation. Through the forms, one becomes one with the eternal Tao and realizes that everything has no beginning or ending, and the practitioner becomes lost within himself in the practice of Ch'i Kung and the related martial arts. This is the reason why many masters will say that they cannot teach one to fight and that one must simply perform his set or forms. In order to fight efficiently, we must first overcome our greatest enemy, and that enemy is ourselves. By performing this meditation in motion, we get to know ourselves and become masters of our own destiny.

Ch'i Kung itself is a method of self defense, and if one masters it, he will not need to seek any other kind of self defense. The Ch'i Kung practitioner, does not need to defend himself, as he is able to take the blow, and if he is injured, he can cure himself in a matter of minutes just by using his mental powers. Ch'i Kung, in this way, is truly a passive self defense art.

The Ch'i Kung practitioner also learns of the nerve spots and joints on the human body. Through this, he knows where to protect himself and where his attacker is most vulnerable. To some extent, other arts have incorporated this system, which is known to the Japanese as atemi and to the Chinese as da muk. However, these systems are rudimentary compared to the system of the Ch'i Kung practice.

Just knowing the nerves and knowing where to hit is only part of the practice. The Ch'i Kung practitioner must learn to harness his internal energy called Ch'i, if he is to be adept at hitting or curing certain nerves and joints. With the aid of this Ch'i, the Ch'i Kung man can paralyze or even kill his attacker. Without this Ch'i, the blows to the nerves and death spots may mean nothing although one can still greatly hurt an attacker in this method. The Ch'i Kung practitioner could also cure the person he has just hurt. It was very necessary for a Ch'i Kung practitioner to be able to both kill and heal. The main view most widely accepted is that the first existing martial art was Ch'i Kung and that all martial arts in China has had their beginnings from Ch'i Kung. Practitioners of Ch'i Kung claim that their art was even pre-Taoist and pre-Buddhist. To be sure, there is no exact evidence existing showing exactly where the martial arts in China came from. However, it is an established fact that the Chinese martial arts are in the thousands. That is to say, that there is no one style of Chinese martial arts, and that they are often paradoxial in connection with one another.

Generally speaking, the Chinese have named their martial arts after certain aspects of the world and universe. For example, the Chinese have styles named after philosophical ideas such as T'ai Ch'i (Grand Ultimate), Pa Kua (Eight Trigrams), Hsing I (From of the Mind), and so on. The Chinese also have styles named after animals such as, Tong Long Pai (Praying Mantis Style), and Pak Hok Pai (White Crane Style). Furthermore, they have styles named after men such as, Pak Mei Pai (White Eyebrow Style), Fat Pai (Priest Style), Wing Chun (named after a woman named Yim Wing Chun). There exist many many more, and that is what makes the Chinese martial arts so very colorful.

As an ending note, we must realize that the practice of Ch'i Kung as applied to the martial arts, places one in a different perspective. Fighting is for children. It is quite easy for one person to overcome another by pure force, but this does not make a man more superior to another simply because he is stronger and able to defeat someone weaker. Ch'i Kung aids the martial artist in guiding him along the path of the righteous and superior man.

How can one learn to win if one has not known defeat? An art is useless if it does not aid one in prolonging one's life and providing good for the world. Indeed, in ancient times, it was quite valid to learn martial arts solely for the sake of fighting. In those days, it was a necessity, but today, this need should be given a lesser role in this society of mankind. No matter how hard one practices to become a top notch fighter, there will come a time when he must be defeated by someone who is better. It is the Way of the Tao.

Let us use these arts to give one a healthy life, and inner happiness, rather than to maim and destroy. If one is to die correctly and bravely, then let one first learn how to live correctly within the overwhelming storm of life. This is one of the noble goals of the practice of Ch'i Kung, and should complement every martial artist's life.

Chapter 12: Ch'i kung:
A needed development

Ch'i King is the art of mastering the unseen life force, but it is more than the development of our energy or life force. It is a way of living one's best in health, mind and spirit. Ch'i Kung stimulates the organs into proper functioning and brings the entire system into balance for optimum performance. Ch'i Kung puts one in communication with one's self and brings about harmony of the mind and body, then harmony with the external order of things. In short, Ch'i Kung harmonizes and fine tunes the human instrument for the greatest possible production and enjoyment.

The Ch'i Kung discipline developed in China about 4000 years ago. It uses slow defined movements coordinated with a particular method of breathing and relaxed concentration. It uses slow movements because slow movements requires and develops control, concentration and awareness.

Because of the structure of the body, certain movements when coordinated with the breathing makes possible very deep inhalation and exhalation. This brings about a cleansing action which readies the body system for oxygen, then through a special breathing technique, this waiting system is filled with a fresh charge of oxygen.

Ch'i Kung having its bases in ideas parallel to Taoism, emphasizes naturalness and harmony — harmony of the body within itself, with the external and harmony of the mind. Through emphasizing naturalness, Ch'i Kung teaches one to become aware of and to act according to the needs and wishes of the body.

The body has many self regulating mechanisms. When the blood sugar level is low, one becomes hungry for food. Food restores this level. When a woman is pregnant she needs certain minerals and nutrients. The self regulating mechanisms will cause her to crave certain foods that will provide her with what she needs even without her knowing that they will.

Ch'i Kung calls upon these such self regulating mechanisms to create a balance in the body. For instance, through proper practice of Ch'i Kung, the digestive system becomes attuned to the needs of the body. When one masters the art of Ch'i Kung, there is no need to fast or overeat in order to force a loss or gain in weight because it is naturally regulated.

Ch'i Kung practice relaxes the tensions in the mind and body. Through gentle meditative movements, ones thoughts flow inward and outward and one is put into a state of calmness and tranquility. One gains even temperment and even blood pressure. This tranquility differs from drug sedation. Sedatives generally reduce neural activity. Ch'i Kung is not like a sedative in that a Ch'i Kung practioner may be relaxed physically, but very alert and awake mentally. Ch'i Kung quiets the nervous system, reduces the blood pressure and respiratory rate, and calms one without interfering with normal mental functions.

At times, as one does the exercise, one is required to concentrate on different parts of the body and to imagine certain activities. Through such imaginings, portions of the body in which we normally do not have control over are stimulated and made to function as they should.

The practice of Ch'i Kung improves blood circulation and enriches the blood with more red blood cells. This increases the supply of oxygen to the tissues and promotes healthier tissues and organs.

The greater supply of oxygon enables the heart to pump slower, yet still provide enough oxygen to the body. Imbalances such as high blood pressure and rapid heart beat are made normal.

Ch'i Kung makes the blood vessels larger and more flexible. This lowers the blood pressure. Ch'i Kung does this by exercising the blood vessels through breath control and gymnastics. After one has mastered Ch'i Kung, one can control heartbeat through developed breath control. Ch'i Kung also keeps the blood vessels clean by properly balancing the diet by regulating the foods wanted.

The Ch'i Kung master has control over his Ch'i and thus has great healing powers. If he has a cut or a bruise, he will concentrate his white blood cells around the wound and prevent infection. Because his blood is rich in red blood cells and oxygen, the wound heals quickly.

Ch'i Kung serves the body as a whole rather than one specific area although this is possible through specialized techniques. Ch'i Kung is also the most natural way of attaining good health and peace of mind. Acupuncture, herbs and medicines are external cures and cures that are really temporary fixatives. Ch'i Kung calls on no external means. Ch'i Kung first of al exercises the internal organs and put them into high running order and balance with each other. This puts the body into a high state of health and enables one to ward off illnesses. If illness does occur, Ch'i Kung causes the body to produce antibodies as it would if it were injected with vaccines or stimulated by an accupuncturist's needle. Ch'i Kung accomplishes this by selective control of the antibody producing mechanisms of the body. The minutest mechanisms of chemistry and tissues are under the control of Ch'i Kung masters. The Ch'i Kung masters rarely becomes sick. If sickness occurs, it will be slight and will not last for long.

Medicine and herbs are indirect cures. They are introduced into the body. Acupuncture too, is an indirect cure because a needle is introduced into the body. It is more direct than medicines however, since it stimulates the body into production of antibodies. Because Ch'i Kung introduces nothing and depends only upon the body to create antibodies; it is the most natural and direct method of cure.

Ch'i Kung is a very sophisticated discipline in which one may spend a year, ten years or a lifetime. But the benefits gained by its practitioners have kept it alive and developing for nearly 4000 years.

PART II

Chapter 1: Principles of ch'i kung

The oldest creation myth of China begins with Chaos. At this time, the three primary elements of the universe — force, form, and substance — were undivided. Then came the great inception, which seperated force from chaos. Force was the purest of the three elements. Later, there came the great beginning, which separated form from chaos. From was an impure element, because form contained energy, and could not exist without it. Last of all came the great homogeneity which made substance visible. Substance was the crudest element because substance contained force and form, and could not exist without them. Then the light and pure substances rose up and formed the heavens, while the heavier and impure substances sank and formed the earth.

Even before this myth of creation, however, the Chinese had assumed the division of all things into Yin and Yang. Force. form, and substance were each divided into Yin and Yang. But the Yin and Yang came before the great divisions and are higher than the three elements. The Harmony of the universe, which is made up of the three elements, depends on the harmony of Yin and Yang.

Yin and Yang originally meant Darkness and Light. But many qualities can be attributed to them. They may be considered lower and higher, inner and outer, water and fire, earth and heavens, man and woman, and non-action and action. Yin and Yang, however, are not distinct, separate qualities.

There is nothing in the universe that is not both Yin and Yang. When we say that something is Yang, it is not purely Yang. Man is called Yang because he is primarily so. But man is both, as male is Yang, and female is Yin. A single male is both Yin and Yang. His exterior is mostly Yang and his interior mostly Yin. Even on the inside, his organs can be either Yin or Yang. An organ itself is Yin on the inside and Yang on the outside. Yin and

Yang are in everything, and they are even in each other.

In the practice of Ch'i Kung, one learns the harmony of the Yin and the Yang. If the Yin and the Yang are in harmony, then the body and the mind are in harmony. Man, like the universe, is made up of the three elements. He has force, and substance. Ch'i Kung teaches one to balance the Yin and Yang of each. Simply stated, one does this by following the way of nature, or the harmony of Yin and Yang.

Ch'i Kung exercises are mainly concerned with form. Form is the element that is the most accessible to training and conditioning. Also, because form is between force and substance, it is the most relevant to each. It is the key to each of the other elements. By mastering form, one has mastered force and substance.

There are many forms in the practice of Chi Kung. All are directed towards the goal of achieving perfect harmony. They are based on the four principles of Ch'i Kung which are: relaxation, tranquality, concentration, and motion.

These principles are the natural modes of life. Individually or in combination they emcompass all the activities of man. Tranquility and relaxation are of the Yin, and concentration and motion are of the Yang. Concentration balances relaxation and tranquility balances motion. When applied correctly, these principles of Ch'i Kung will bring one into harmony with Yin and Yang.

One must understand that the four principles are not separate from one another. Just as Yin is in Yang and Yang is in Yin, the four principles are to some degree mixed with each other. Ch'i Kung is an art of harmony and unity. All is one, and therefore it is difficult to separate it into parts.

The four principles must be understood if one is to practice correctly. They are explained briefly below.

Relaxation plays a very important part in the practice of Ch'i Kung. When we talk of relaxation or not using strength, we do not mean a total limpness of the body, with the composure of a wet mop. This relaxation means to expand and contract the body by alternately tensing and relaxing the muscles. This expanding and contracting serves to produce heat which is conducive to the formation of the unseen life force. Also, when we mention tension, this is not to be confused with the type of tension one gets after a hard day's work, but this is tension or strength used wisely in the right amounts coupled with correct concentration in order to achieve tranquility.

The second principle of Ch'i Kung is the attainment of tranquility. This tranquility may be described as a calmness within motion and movement. One must seek stillness of mind even when the body functions and flows from movement to movement. During the average person's waking hours, his brain burns up much energy. If this energy is not replaced, he feels fatigued and overworked. Ch'i Kung practice serves to replenish and store this vital energy when one practices correctly. Furthermore, Ch'i Kung helps to regulate this expenditure of energy so one uses just the right amount of energy for the tasks at hand and does not waste the precious life force. Tranquility does not mean rest, it means to be aware of yourself in a silent manner.

One must remember that motion leads to concentration, and relaxation leads to tranquility. Furthermore, relaxation and tranquility must be practiced at the same time.

Correct concentration will bring one into harmony with the unseen life force. Concentration with movement will bring about an improvement of the functions of the brain in that one will be able to relax more fully. This will bring about serenity which will further lead one to fuller concentration. This will assist body and organ functions and enable one to realize a greater Ch'i, or original energy, potential.

The last principle is that motion must be natural. One must not force or overpractice in the art of Ch'i Kung for it is possible to injure oneself. At first, the movements will feel awkward and unnatural, but by constant practice and diligence, the body and mind will be accustomed to the movements and thus, the practice of Ch'i Kung will become natural. One must feel comfortable, and one must take care to use just the right amount of force, concentration, relaxation and tranquility. The whole point here is that one should not go to extremes in the practice of Ch'i Kung or in anything else for that matter.

THE INWARD AND OUTWARD MODES OF MOTION

In the art of Ch'i Kung, there are two modes of motion, the inward and the outward. The inward motion may be thought of as the mental energy of concentration which is integrated with physical action. The practitioner of Ch'i Kung does not act without awareness. The mind and body work together, each aware of the other. When a person speaks, he unconsciously moves his hands to tell the same story in the language of hands. In Ch'i Kung, one learns the unity of mind and body that the mouth and hand have. The inward motion is the mental counterpart of each physical action, and the outward motion is the physical counterpart of each mental action. The concept of the unity of inward and outward motion is a basic one underpinning much of Chinese medical theory, especially in acupuncture.

Tranquility is not only a part of inward motion, but is a part of outward motion as well. Tranquility, as described earlier, is not a state of unconscious relaxation, but a state of quiet awareness. It cannot be forced, it must be attained by the natural action of controlled inhalation and exhalation. In this state, the mind is very still and one notices the smallest movement in himself and his surroundings. One is aware of the dropping leaf although he does not lose his concentration and does not stir. In tranquility, the body and mind are quiet and yet very aware. Tranquility is of mind and body, and thus is a part of both inward and outward modes. Tranquility in action and thought lends an assurance and a calmness which is a sign of Ch'i Kung.

THE IMPORTANCE OF RESPIRATORY CONTROL

The importance of inhaling and exhaling correctly cannot be overstressed in that it is necessary to the conduction of the vital energy. This energy can be divided into two types, the internal and the external. The two types of energy may be thought of as mental and physical energy, respectively. Concentration and movement are important in that they influence correct breathing and thus affect the activities of the vital energy. Correct breathing, in turn, helps to attain harmony between concentration and motion.

Concentration through meditation reaches tranquility. Similarly, movements are conjoined with the breathing cycles to reach a perfect physical balance where they operate as one. One must learn to contemplate on the areas around one's navel in order to induce the flow of energy and to reach harmony with the Ch'i. This cannot be forced and must be reached naturally like the sailboat which flows with the wind currents. It is important to remember that the elements of Ch'i Kung are all interrelated, and that progress in one aspect will help the whole.

In order to inhale and exhale properly, one must follow certain forms and positions. Breathing must be done gently, continuously, and evenly. In other words, the length of time for exhaling and inhaling must be extended much like the weaving of the silkworm. This is why some forms in Ch'i Kung breathing control were named the Art of the Eight Silken Forms. The cultivation of the inner energy is very vital for the protection of the inner organs. Thus, the practice of Ch'i Kung not only gives the mind discipline, but helps to store and send the viral force to various points on the body through methodical use and correct procedure.

THE HARMONY OF ACTION AND NON-ACTION, OR OF MOTION AND TRANQUILITY

Ch'i Kung practice enables one to understand the way of life and to live in harmony with it. One in harmony lives life on a higher level. In order to understand the way of life, one must understand the balance between action and non-action. This is accomplished by balancing the four principles of Ch'i Kung. Motion is balanced by tranquility and relaxation by concentration. Correct practice of Ch'i Kung enables one to balance these forces of action and non-action.

Chinese physicians believed that a long and peaceful life depended on good circulation and the even flowing of Ch'i. Equilibrium of Ch'i allows one to live in harmony. The Chinese medical texts explain that, "In order to balance the Yin and Yang, let the harmony,

50

through the Ch'i activities, assist the blood circulation." Through the Ch'i activities, one also learns to relax the muscles, and joints and to cultivate original vitality.

Chinese physicians say "When the body is in disharmony, sickness occurs. This pertains to the spiritual as well. From psychological disturbances, the physiological processes are directly influenced, and this will bring on sickness." Through the practice of Ch'i activities, these imbalances can be corrected and the human body restored to harmony with nature as it should be.

If action and non-action are not balanced properly, one should not expect changes for the better. Chinese texts explain that if the blood vessels are damaged, the circulation of the blood will be hindered, and the Ch'i is prevented from flowing easily. This is akin to a water pipe in that if the pipe is in disuse, the water does not flow correctly. Too much non-action has destroyed its utility. In order to maintain the blood vessels, one must follow the principle of motion and tranquility, or action and non-action. Then the circulation of Ch'i will be vigorous and the Yin and Yang harmonious.

In the practice of Ch'i Kung, it is important to realize that motion and tranquility cannot be separated, and in order to realize the full potential of Ch'i Kung training, these two features must be blended together. This is indeed difficult to understand, for if one can realize tranquility, then he will know how to perform the correct movements in a flowing manner. Certain movements and actions in Ch'i Kung will stress either motion or silence, but in general, Ch'i Kung covers all human activity; that is to say, that the forms cover lying, sitting, and standing positions.

Ch'i Kung is a fine foundation for the learning and application of other arts. It is of special interest to those who practice the martial arts in that it will help to improve their understanding of their arts, and help to combine the unseen life force of Ch'i Kung with their practices.

Traditionally Ch'i Kung requires practice at least twice a day. It was suggested that one should practice during noon time, and at midnight, but this is very difficult to do today. For this day and age, it is advisable that one practices in the morning and again at night. However, one should use common sense in planning a set schedule. In most cases, it is best to practice the art of tranquility first and then practice the art of motion.

When one practices, it is extremely important to empty the part of the body which is above the navel, and to fill the part below the navel. In other words, one must sink his Ch'i to that area below the navel in order for it to flow correctly, and correctly center one's point of gravity.

The practice of Ch'i Kung can be compared to cooking. If the food prepared is overdone or overcooked, it does not taste good. So too, the Ch'i Kung practitioner must take care to practice just enough so that he will not be "overdone" or "overcooked." In other words, don't try to be too fanatical in practice or be too unconcerned about progress, as both will hinder one's progress. One's practice must be done in a circular fashion. That is, movements are circular and progress is to be found through a cyclical pattern of exercises which are continous.

Chapter 2: Practice of ch'i kung

Ch'i Kung possesses a very close relationship to Nature and the life processes. Ch'i Kung influences the forces of nature and thus influences the movements and changes in life. Ch'i Kung does this through breath control and gymastic exercises.

In the practice of Ch'i Kung, it is difficult to separate one thing from another. Everything is done together as one. The movements, correct meditation, and breathing are all done at the same time. It is all Ch'i Kung. For the sake of clarity, each aspect will be explained separately. The reader must remember, however, that they are practiced together.

Breathing control is the most important aspect of Ch'i Kung. Through proper breathing, the organs of the body are strengthened, and their functioning is improved. Inhaling brings nourishment into the body and assists blood circulation and organ function. Exhaling serves to cleanse the body of harmful elements and wastes.

In order to inhale and exhale properly, one must follow certain forms and positions. Breathing must be done gently, continuously, and evenly. The length of time for exhaling and inhaling must be extended much like the weaving of the silkworm.

The importance of inhaling and exhaling correctly cannot be overstressed. Breath control is necessary for the conduction of the ch'i or vital energy. Vital energy is both mental and physical energy. Correct breathing allows the vital energy to flow naturally. With practice, one can control the flow of energy and direct it to different parts of the body.

By breath control, the rate of breathing can be lowered. The practitioner needs to breathe only 4 or 5 times a minute, instead of the average 15 to 20 times.

X-ray photographs have shown that the practitioner of Ch'i Kung has lungs that are larger than the ordinary person's. Because of breath control, and increased lung capacity, one can lower the level of breathing.

By this method, strength is conserved and energy is used efficiently. This can be compared to an oil lamp. A good oil lamp uses little oil but produces much light. Ch'i Kung teaches the human body to burn life slowly but keep the same amount of light. Breath control conserves energy and yet gives much nourishment to the body.

The main principle of Ch'i Kung is control of the energy centers above and below the navel. The Ch'i in these centers can be cultivated through correct breathing control and meditation. Each breath must be swallowed and forced down to these centers. In this way, the ch'i is nourished.

One must be like a tree. The bottom half of the tree is sturdy and firmly rooted. Rainstorms do not wash it away. The Ch'i is found in centers below the navel. By concentrating the ch'i into the lower part of the body, one becomes as immovable as a tree.

The tree limbs and branches are flexible. They bend to the wind but do not break. By making the upper part of the body light and relaxed, one will be able to move gracefully and efficiently. He will be strong and immovable and at the same time, light and flexible. Like the tree, one will be able to weather the storms of life with little wear and tear on the body.

During the practice of Ch'i Kung, one empties the center above the navel and fills the center below the navel with Ch'i. In this way, one becomes like the tree. To do this, one must use concentration and breath control. One must concentrate on the center of the body and consciously think of the strength or Ch'i being lowered.

One begins by concentrating on a spot about three inches inside the body just in back of the navel. Then one lowers the spot of concentration to about three inches below the navel. Meditation on this point will nourish the body energy. This point is called the Ch'i Hai.

The area around the navel is called the Tan Tien. The two major centers of energy are called the Ch'i Hai and the Kuan Yuan. The Ch'i Hai, which means "the Ocean of Ch'i" is of great importance because it is like the ocean. This point contains a great abundance of Ch'i, like the ocean has a great abundance of water. The Kuan Yuan, which means "the Great Constitution" is of importance because much Ch'i is produced here. By concentrating on these two points, one creates energy. Concentration also aids in the circulation of oxygen, which is needed to create and nourish the body energy.

The energy from the navel can be conducted to various parts of the body. First year practitioners learn to conduct the energy up the back, over the head, into the chest, through the arms, and into the hands. One knows that he is practicing correctly if he feels heat in the palm of his hands. Experienced practitioners can produce visible steam from their fingertips. This is because much Ch'i has been concentrated into the hands.

Another important point is Ming Men, which means "the Gate of Life," and is found at the base of the spine. By concentrating on this point, one will produce heat and give a general feeling of well being. This heat is similar to boiling water. It will produce perspiration and cleanse the body. Ch'i Kung differs from other types of physical recreation because one perspires just enough and does not become soaking wet. One should not over perspire because then one can catch a cold. The Ch'i Kung practitioner practices only enough to cleanse his system thoroughly.

Life is like the blossoming of a flower. People are born, grow, and die. How one grows and matures depend on how one takes care of himself during the youthful stages of life. People who have not cared for their health complain of aches and pains. They have heavy head and light feet which results in the unbalancing of the human body in later life. This condition is not limited to elderly people. Young people often have this condition too which results in being temperatmental, and in lacking self-control. As a result of being emotionally and psychologically disturbed, their bodies begin to deteriorate. Conditions like ulcers and poor blood circulation come about. These conditions can be avoided by taking care of oneself. This can be achieved by the practice of Ch'i Kung.

When the body is in harmony, the practitioner becomes more aware of himself. He achieves a type of "inner hearing" that is attuned to the Tao. This consciousness of life brings an awareness of how to live life more harmoniously.

There are 152 forms of Ch'i Kung and more than 1,000 sequences. Some forms are simple and others are complex. Certain individuals will like certain forms and dislike others. If one is not comfortable following some of the forms, one should change the forms or sequences to suit their taste. When one is just beginning, it is best to follow the instructor as closely as possible. In time, one will develop an individual style.

Certain exercises in Ch'i Kung help to improve certain physical weaknesses. It is up to the individual to find out where he needs improvement. By concentrating on the Ch'i Kung exercises that help to cure these weaknesses, the practitioner will be rid of these problems. Instructors will inform students of what exercise effects what weakness.

In order to learn and remember the forms, one must be relaxed and take one step at a time. It is important that one not use too much force in performing complicated movements. The beginner should take everything slowly and easily. Ten minutes to half an hour, twice daily, is sufficient practice for the novice. Take the practice in a serious and patient manner. Do not be discouraged if no progress is felt. One must keep on trying for the road is long and full of curves and obstructions.

Ch'i Kung is nourishment for the body that gives strength, energy, and awareness. It is one of the most important practices in Chinese medicine. But one should remember that too much practice can be harmful. It is not correct to practice all day and then rest for 100 days. One should practice just enough each day on a regular basis. By practicing just enough, the body will be nourished and exhaustion and everyday fatigue will pass away.

Ch'i Kung brings out the unseen power that lies within all of us. Because most people are unaware of this power, they do not exercise it regularly. It remains hidden and uncultivated. Ch'i Kung brings out this power, and strengthens the organs and human body as a whole.

One will not see benefits in one day or one night. Anything that is worthwhile in life takes a little longer. As the old saying goes, "As you sow, so shall you reap." One minute's practice will give you one minute's harvest, and one hour's practice will give one hour's harvest. Like the bamboo, it takes time to center the strength to the root in order to withstand the wind and the rain.

Don't expect too much too soon. There will be results if you practice according to the instructor's orders. If the roots are healthy, the leaves and limbs will be healthy, and the flowers will blossom beautifully. The Chinese say that, "When the waters accumulate together, it becomes a lake, when it flows together, it becomes the ocean." So if you practice everyday, soon you will be like the ocean, and you will cultivate the great reservoir of Ch'i.

You must devote yourself to Ch'i Kung, and make an effort to practice everyday. This is the first rule that every practitioner must follow. The unseen life force cannot be cultivated by part-time or once a week practice. Dedication to practice is one of the keys to success in this ancient art.

How long one practices depends on the individual. If one is already in fine health, then this person should concentrate on building up and storing Ch'i. Usually this would only take one practice set. One can choose to practice the sitting, standing, or prone set. If you practice all three, it takes about three hours which is impractical in this day and age. Therefore, one should practice only one of the three each day. On the weekends, one should practice all three. For invalids, who want to practice to improve their recovery, they should practice in short sets three or four times a day. Ten to thirty minute sets are sufficient.

The place where one practices should be a quiet place with an abundance of fresh air. If one has a mountain retreat, one should go there at least once a year or every three months. One should try to practice even if it is noisy because it will help to improve discipline and improve concentration. If you practice indoors, make sure that the place is not dusty and there is sufficient ventilation. Never practice in the rain because it will hinder the flow of Ch'i which comes from the inside out. It is ideal to practice outdoors in natural surroundings of trees, plants, and flowers. When practicing outdoors, during the summer, be careful to avoid the noon sun. In ancient times, practitioners were required to practice under the noon sun. For beginners, however, this practice is not suitable. During the winter, do not let drafts of cold wind blow directly onto one's face, or inside one's nose or mouth. Drafts will completely destroy one's concentration and breathing. Traditionally, short hair was required for Ch'i Kung practice because long hair distracts one's concentration when the wind is blowing. Long hair also interferes with certain movements. Short hair was also required due to certain religions and philosophical practices at the time. If you should decide to cut your hair, however, use common sense and don't try to be fanatical about it.

Before the practice of Ch'i Kung, make sure that all work and other daily needs are accomplished. This will put one at ease. Wear loose clothing preferably light in weight. The best thing to wear is a light robe.

Do not eat too much before practice because it will fill up the stomach. If you are tired, sick, or hungry, do not engage in practice. If one's emotions are upset, do not engage in practice.

Women may practice during menstruation unless they feel uncomfortable. In these cases, practice should be terminated until recovery is complete.

Ch'i Kung should be practiced on a scheduled basis. There is a time for every activity in life. The practice of Ch'i Kung should be done daily at the same time.

Chapter 3: Sensations felt during practice

During the practice of Ch'i Kung, one will invariably feel different things; mentally and physically. The following is an explanation of the various symptoms:

Flowing of the Body Energy
The most common symptom to experience is an increase of body heat in the abdomen. Most practitioners agree that it comes from the inside out, and that this takes place especially when one is in a tranquil state. This means that there is an increase in the flow of the unseen life force due to correct concentration on the area of the Ch'i Hai. One can also feel the stomach throbbing like a miniature drum. This indicates that the stomach and intestines are being cleansed and that the digestion is being regulated.

Peace & Comfort
Another sensation is one of peace and comfort. This happens when the practitioner is exercising or meditating. One feels warm on the inside because the Ch'i is circulating. The novice is perplexed because he thinks he should be warm on the outside also. This is not true because the energy is stored inside. One does not feel warm on the outside until he uses the energy in physical activity. This is a good sign as it shows that the novice has learned to create and store the Ch'i.

Tingling
A tingling sensation may be felt on the skin during practice. This feeling is attributed to the circulation of the Ch'i. It is usually felt when one is in a full state of tranquility.
If one feels his heart is beating too fast, then one is too tense. The neck muscles are not

relaxed, and the breathing is unnatural. All one needs to do is to relax and go back to breathing naturally.

Increase of Saliva

There should be an increase of saliva if one is practicing correctly. The saliva aids the digestive system and helps internal organs to function better. Correct inhalation and exhalation and the loosening up of the body joints produces the increase of saliva.

Heaviness due to incorrect breathing control

Sometimes one feels his stomach is heavy and bloated. This is due to one's concentrating on the lower stomach too much and holding one's breath too long. By relaxing and breathing naturally, the feeling will pass. If one feels heavy all over, and his head feels congested; one is too tense and may be forcing himself. To settle this feeling, one must sit down, take it easy, and do some deep breathing. If the body feels like a thousand pounds, the concentration is too rigid and the breathing is irregular. Taking long and short breaths creates an uneven circulation of oxygen and energy. One should breathe naturally and lessen his concentration. This condition may cause stiffness in the shoulders. One may remedy this by performing some circular arm exercises.

Thirst of Dryness

If one feels thirsty or has a dry throat; then one is either breathing through the mouth or closing the mouth too tight. To ride oneself of this problem, just drink a little water or regulate the breathing.

Visual Phenomena

One will experience unusual visual phenomena while engaged in Ch'i Kung practice. Colors, lights, and steam are some of the experiences and these happenings have special significances. There is no need to fear any of this for it is quite natural when one has reached a height of tranquility. These experiences do not last long. There will be a text to explain the significance of these happenings in the future; but, for the present, it is beyond the scope of this book. Generally speaking, these happenings are akin to the dream states and experiences. There are some who believe that incorrect practice of Ch'i Kung is harmful and can bring on illness or psychic degeneration. But according to the beliefs of the author, this is purely superstitious nonsense. If one does not practice correctly, one has simply exercised and nothing more. One still benefits. The so called supernatural experiences can be explained logically and should not be feared. One should try Ch'i Kung with an open mind before condemning or praising it.

One should never practice when one is upset and breathing control should not be forced. The opposite results will occur if one forces himself.

Dizziness

A novice may experience dizziness in the beginning stages of practice. This feeling is natural. In time, the dizziness will pass. If one does not feel anything, he should stop and analyze to see what he is doing incorrectly. One must feel an even flow of energy through mind and body. As in all arts, correct practice depends on the individual.

The important thing to realize is that one cannot force these conditions to come about; if the student is patient and diligent, all these conditions will come in time. The more one looks forward to gaining something, the less chance it will take place. There are also many sensations of comfort. One will feel like being in the wintertime with the sun shining in one's eyes and the snow melting. One feels warm and refreshed.

A deep and full rest at night is another fine condition that can be attained with the practice of Ch'i Kung. Because of this practice, a person will need less sleep than usual. He will awake a new person, replenished, and ready to face a brand new day.

After Ch'i Kung practice, one will feel stronger and more energetic and the mind will feel clear and tranquil. After prolonged training, one will feel light but strong. One may not even be aware of a physical body and everything seems like a calm lake.

Chapter 4: Experience of a ch'i kung practitioner

Quite often Ch'i-kung practitioners will be treated to strange and fascinating experiences — experiences which are sometimes perplexing and very moving.

These experiences occur when one is in a state of tranquility and relaxed awareness and are manifested through any combination of senses. One may see vivid patterns of brilliantly colored lights, hear strange but beautiful sounds and rhythm or feel emersed in a sea of warmth and well being.

Actual accounts are numerous and varied but always interesting. One 23 years old student who has been practicing for five months describes her personal experiences in Ch'i-kung in the following manner:

> *In my attempt to write about my involvement with Ch'i Kung these past six months, I have come to realize that relating my personal experience would be limited by what little knowledge I have of the concepts and philosophy underlying this art and by the use of words which oftentimes cannot convey the full extent of what a person experiences. Realizing these limitations, I can only hope that the reader will gain some understanding of Ch'i Kung.*
>
> *Ch'i Kung has been for me an enlightening and fulfilling experience. It is because Ch'i Kung encompasses and emphasizes the totality of the individual-his mind and body, the physical and the spiritual. Each is related to the other, each complements the other. Unlike Western philosophy which to me emphasizes the external, Ch'i Kung is focusing on the internal, looking and listening to the*

internal, becoming aware and understanding what is happening inside of you. Through the breathing, the movements and concentration one becomes aware of the strength and energy within. It is an internal strength which flows and is very much a part of one's being. It is an internal strength which is developed by moving, flowing with the forces within one's body.

At first it was difficult for me to understand this concept of internal strength for everything was very now to me. As I progressed however, I became aware of changes within my body and of the sensations which have become a part of my experience with Chi Kung. A great deal of emphasis is placed on breathing or what is called "reverse breathing". This is the foundation of what one experiences when meditating or going through the movements. It is through breathing that I have been very aware of the internal strength within me. It is through breathing that one nurtures and develops and is made more intensely aware of this internal life force called "Ch'i". In doing the breathing exercises I find an inner peace and calmness. My mind is clear and I can feel and see what is happening within. My whole being becomes immersed in this experience and there have been times when I have been flashes of color — yellow-gold, blue, green, orange. Sometimes these colors appear as band; othertimes as flashes of colors and in veils of color.

All else is hazy except of that one point of concentration. As I breath I can feel the air go down to the area below my navel. It seems at times that I am breathing without control and that by body is doing everything. In inhaling the air goes down to the lower abdomen. In exhaling, the air goes further down. At the same time I can feel sensation of heat and a kind of tingling in my arms and palms of my hands. Time passes but I am not aware of it. I am in me and not in the external world. As time progressed these experiences became more intense and happened much more quickly than in the beginning. It is a very strange feeling to know that you are alive and breathing existing in the world and yet, at the same time experiencing such a feeling of wholeness and oneness with yourself that the external world does not exist. You exist and you are a vital life force. You possess a life energy and are one with it. In doing the movements I became aware of how natural and how wonderful it is to move with and flow with the internal energy within. You feel your body alive with this vitality and energy and flow with it. You let your body's life force guide and lead you and become so aware of the naturalness, the flowing within. It is as if your arms and legs, your whole body were being controlled by some unknown force which seems unreal. But you are aware and you know that this force is you. Again, you become one, you are one flowing and moving so naturally in tune to the force within. Nothing else exists but you. You move ever so slowly letting yourself flow within. The movements become and are manifestations of what is happening within. You are moving slowly and yet you feel this tremendous energy move within you. It is as if some electric current was running through your body and you feel a tremendous amount of heat in your palms. It is difficult to understand or to fully grasp this concept of being able to move so slowly and yet at the same time feel the movement, the vitality within your body. At that moment you are calm and vibrant at the one instant. In my fifth month of Chi Kung, I had an intense experience while going through the movements, an experience I shall never forget. Prior to that evening I had experienced the sensations of heat and flowing electric-like energy while practicing. But that evening in my fifth month was different. I became more immersed in experiencing myself than I had ever been before. My breathing was very deep and very slow. It was not breathing at all. Then I became aware of a golden light in front of me and soon the golden light became an aura about my body. As I began the movements I felt a gush of warmth flow through my hands to my palms. My arms were tingling and prickling with a sensation that seemed to be flowing from my lower abdomen to my arms. I was moving very, very slowly. I was beginning to wonder if I were moving at all. I could feel the sensations move in tune with my breathing. As I looked at my hands I could see waves of heat like those coming from a hot asphalt road. As I continued with the movements while standing up I could feel the warmth go down through my legs as I exhaled and finally reach the bottom of my feet. It was here that I could feel a tingling sensation. All this was happening while I moved ever so slowly. The energy I felt was so very strong and yet I felt calm and clear in my mind and body. Since this experience such sensations have been consistent and of great intensity. I am always amazed to realize how much time passes but how time seems to stand still.

As a result of my involvement with Ch'i Kung, I feel stronger, more alive and very aware of my body. Through Ch'i Kung I have gained an inner calmness and strength which are so important to me. I have come to understand the workings of my body and gained a deeper appreciation of the messages my body conveys to me. But much more important is the appreciation and deep respect I have for the intricate relationship between my physical and spiritual being. It is a relationship which all of us need to become aware of and appreciate. It is the essence of man which is not fully understood by the Western way of thinking. It is a oneness and completeness which exists in man and I have been very fortunate to have experienced this thus far. I feel I have so much to learn and understand and hopefully I will.

Christine Sueda
August 28, 1972.

Such experiences are a natural result of certain movements which exercise the mind. Movements of the arms or body are not merely movements of the arms or body alone. They are also movements of the mind or thoughts inward and outward.

What occurs can be thought of as conscious dreaming. The mind settles at a level of awareness somewhere between consciousness and dreaming. When conscious, one is generally aware of this surroundings and is able to choose what he sees.

In contrast, when dreaming one is generally not aware of his surroundings and does not choose what he "sees". In the "conscious dream" state, while one is aware of his surroundings as when conscious he has no control over what he "sees" as in dreaming.

A recent observation by Western psychologists is that conditions of life and society force us to develop certain senses, awareness and sensitivity at the expense of others. Education and communication place emphasis on sight and sound. And sight and sound are becoming increasingly overhelming in variety and intensity. A result is that we are

64

becoming increasingly deaf to the very subtle.

The brain at all times communicate with every part of the human body. This enables self regulation, proper functioning and self preservation. However, much body information do not enter our normal stream of thought and become concious to us because they are not necessary for our conscious activities. Much body consciousness of this type have long been lost to most of us.

The concentration resulting from Ch'i Kung shuts out distractions and enables one to look into one's self. Awareness becomes manifested in light and sound and feelings.

The Chinese explain that the colored lights one sees in Ch'i Kung meditation reflects one's pattern of internal being — one's inner condition or state. The music is mind music and reflects the harmony within. The heart and other body rhythms manifests itself as music.

Each particular experience has its own significance in terms of internal state or condition. But in general, harmonious sounds indicate well being while disharmonious sounds indicate disharmony. Purple or dark colors reflect disturbance within and without, and it is a serious warning. Comfortable colors are good. It should be noted here that the "I Ching" mentions orange-yellow light as an indicator of the best condition. One should remember this color was mentioned earlier as having being the Imperial Color ever since the Yellow Emperor, Huang Ti.

Comfortable colors represent the first stages for beginners, and each stage is represented by a different color. In addition to color, there are different types of light, but the beginner need only learn about two — the Yin Light and the Yang Light.

The Yang Light radiates from one's front. It approaches, passes through the body and surrounds one. It is an external light showing well being between the body and the external. It is not an infrequent experience to serious beginners.

The Yin Light radiates from within and may pass out and around one's self. It is an internal light, warm and comfortable. The Yin Light, however, is quite rare and it almost never occurs to beginners. It is the property of masters with highly developed Ch'i. Energy from within radiates outward and under a particular combination of internal body and external weather conditions charges the air in a way not unlike static electricity and manifests itself as a visible glow — a glow and light which can be seen by others.

Chapter 5: Ch'i kung and the functioning of the organs

THE DIGESTIVE SYSTEM

Through proper practice of Ch'i Kung, the digestive system becomes attuned to the needs of the body. If one's weight is not normal, the practice of Ch'i Kung helps to achieve the optimum natural weight by harmonizing eating habits with the needs of the body. When one masters the art of Ch'i Kung, there is no need to fast or overeat in order to force a loss or gain in weight because it is naturally regulated.

Many testimonies could be given on the effectiveness of this art in losing weight without dieting. Christine Sueda, the student whose testimony you read in the preceding chapter, started practising the Art of the Eight Silken Forms in March. Being overweight worried her very much, but by the end of May, she had lost fifteen pounds and felt very comfortable. She, like others, will continue the practice of Ch'i Kung until she reaches her ideal height.

Practical experience has shown that Ch'i Kung breathing leads one to perfect stomach control. Breathing exercises contract and stretch the abdominal muscles. Ch'i Kung assists one in achieving perfect balance of function within the stomach. The stomach's digestive system can be slowed down if one eats too quickly or speeded up if one eats too slowly in order to reach an equilibrium.

Normally, one's stomach contracts when one exhales and expands when one inhales. In order to clear the intestines of waste material, however, one must apply the techniques of reverse breathing.

Saliva and secretion processes are also influenced by Ch'i Kung. An illustrative example of this is an individual wrought with tuberculosis. His saliva and secretion content will be lower than that of an average person. Through the practice and application of Ch'i Kung, these functions can be made to operate normally.

Salty nutrients causes softness of the bones. Muscles and flesh become deficient and the

66

mind becomes despondent. The pulse quickens and complexion becomes sallow. Diseases of the blood and bones should not be treated by salty nutrients. Its usefulness comes in the treatment of sore throats, toothaches, or heart pains. It also helps to make the heart more pliable and strengthens the heart beat. Salt can also be used in draining the kidneys. When using salt treatments, one must use rock salt and not the commercial type.

Too much pungent food will knot the muscles. Fingernails and toenails will become decayed. If there is a weakness of the respiratory tract, do not use pungent food because muscles and pores will be affected for the worse. Pungent foods drain the lungs of all waste and prevent dryness of the kidneys. It helps to open up the pores and facilitates the functioning of saliva and fluid secretions.

Chinese health practices state that food should be chewed to a pulp to assist the functioning of the digestive system. The reason for this is that matter cannot be digested until it has become completely depolarized.

Chinese physicians believe that natural foods are much better for overall improvement of health. However, one shouldn't force oneself to change over into a completely new diet, but should change over gradually especially if one has a health probelm.

Ch'i Kung practice serves to regulate nutrition of the human organism. If one is over-weight, Ch'i Kung practice will curb one's appetite, and one who is underweight will feel his hunger increased so he can gain weight.

Dietetics play a very important role in health. We know that we can treat certain conditions with correct dieting and nutrition. According to Chinese medicine, diet is very important to Ch'i Kung practice. Especially when one is just on the verge of learning Ch'i Kung. The Ch'i Kung expert, however, can dispense with dieting because nutritional needs are already regulated. According to the Chinese medicial science,

>"sour foods toughen the flesh and are injurious to the muscles. Flesh becomes hardened and wrinkled and lips become chapped. Sour foods adversely affect the functioning of the liver. A symptom of improper functioning of the liver due to excessive sour foods is excessive salivation. This doesn't mean that sour food has no use, for it has beneficial affects. Sour foods act as an astringent, and thus prevent tardiness of the heart. In connection with the liver, one uses sour food to drain and expel waste products. Also, if the lungs are weak, sour food will strengthen the lungs and improve breathing. If too much sweet foods are consumed, pain and aches will develop in the bone structures (like arthritis) the heart will be too full

of energy, the kidneys will be unbalanced, and the loss of hair will be imminent. Excessive activity of the liver can be balanced by the consumption of sweets. Sweet foods will also drain and expel waste products from the heart.

An excess of bitter nutrients cause dryness of the spleen and congests stomach activity. Bitter foods also age the skin, and causes body hair to fall out. Diseases of the bone structure should not be treated with bitter foods. When the spleen suffers from too much moisture, bitter foods should be taken. Bitter foods also help to alleviate congestion in the upper respiratory system by dispersing the mucous.

THE CIRCULATORY SYSTEM

The practice of Ch'i Kung has a very beneficial effect on the circulatory system. Imbalances, such as high blood pressure and rapid heart beat, can be made normal. Ch'i Kung enriches blood that is weak in red blood cells. This enables the heart to pump slower and yet provide enough exygen to the body.

Ch'i Kung makes the blood vessels larger and more flexible. This lowers the blood pressure. Ch'i Kung does this by exercising the blood vessels through breath control and gymnastics. After one has mastered Ch'i Kung, one can control heartbeat through developed breath control. Ch'i Kung also keeps the blood vessels clean by properly balancing the diet by regulating the foods wanted.

If there is disharmony in the mind and body, one puts a great strain on the heart. Ch'i Kung practice relaxes the tensions in the mind and body. It does this by balancing the Yin and Yang. One gains even temperament and even blood pressure.

The Ch'i Kung master rarely becomes sick. If sickness occurs, it will be very slight and will not last long. The master has control over his Ch'i and thus has great healing powers. If he has a cut or a bruise, he will concentrate his white blood cells around the wound and prevent infection. Because his blood is rich in red blood cells and oxygen, the would will heal quickly.

OTHER ORGANS

Functions of the brain and nervous system can be controlled by the use of Ch'i Kung. Ch'i Kung is a stabilizing influence on the activities of the brain. It puts one in a state of calmness and tranquility and protects the brain from overstress.

The practice of Ch'i Kung puts one in a tranquil state that differs from drug sedation. Taken in small doses, sedatives make a person less inhibited and are sometimes used in psychotherapy. Sedatives generally increase the threshold of the neurons and thus reduce neural activity. To gain a restful night's sleep, one does not need to take sedatives but only practice Ch'i Kung. Ch'i Kung is not like a sedative in that a Ch'i Kung practitioner may be relaxed physically, but very aware and awake mentally. Ch'i Kung quiets the nervous system, reduces the blood pressure and respiratory rate, and calms one without interfering with the normal mental functions.

There are other differences between Ch'i Kung and medicines. One great difference is that Ch'i Kung is the more natural method of attaining good health and peace of mind. Ch'i Kung serves the body as a whole and not any one specific area although this is possible through specialized Ch'i Kung techniques.

Ancient practitioners used Ch'i Kung to prevent illness, prolong life, and insure good health. These goals are still sought after in today's world. Therefore, Ch'i Kung is a practical means and method of gaining well-being in today's society.

Ch'i Kung practice also helps skin tone by giving rise to a clear and healthful looking complexion. The reason for this is that it helps to balance the electricity of the skin. Ch'i Kung evenly distributes the positive and negative charges in the skin. Ancient practitioners of Chinese health hygiene would say that Ch'i Kung balances the Yin and the Yang of the skin. Ch'i Kung neutralizes the electricity of the skin by regulating the oxygen supply in the blood stream.

Ch'i Kung practice is an excellent self-discipline of mental and physical hygiene. Some illnesses can be completely cured by the practice. A frail person can be made very strong by practicing his art. If one has the patience and preserverance to study and practice Ch'i Kung, practice is a medium to realize the full human potential in all of us. Age and sex are no barriers in the practice of this unique and rare art.

PART III

The art of the Eight Silken Forms

THE ART OF THE EIGHT SILKEN FORMS

Ch'i Kung practice consists of sitting, lying and standing postures of which standing forms are considered to be the most effective. However, after a hard day at work, the sitting forms may be employed to gain the same benefits. The lying movements may be used by an individual after recovering from an operation or serious illness. It is also conducive to relaxation and rest.

Instructions for the Eight Silken Forms in the sitting Positions

Preliminary Instructions

Beginning Meditation for Tranquility Sit with legs arranged in a comfortable position. The back is straight but not rigid and hands are in lap (Women place their right hand on top for men. This is only applicable for meditation. When performing the series of movements, the right hand is on top for both sexes.) Eyes should be fixed at an arbitrary point directly to the center and at a distance of 3 1/2 to 5 feet away. Using "reversed breathing," inhale and exhale nine times. The breathing is an integral part of movements and should eventually come naturally, but some general rules to remember are: exhale when pushing out, inhale when bringing hands in, and change breathing when hands make a change.

FORM I The Blooming of Spring

STEP 1 (photo 1) From the meditative position, slightly raise hands, circle them to the outside and forward rotating wrists so that palms are down. Touch fingertips to knees and then allow hands and arms to sink until entire hands rest on knees.

STEP 3 (photo 3) Push hands forward. Do not extend arms completely but leave elbows slightly bent.

STEP 2 (photo 2) Draw hands back and upward to the shoulders.

STEP 4 (photo 4) Move elbows outward in order to rotate hands inward so that fingers face each other.

1

2

3

4

STEP 5 (photo 5) Slightly bend elbows to move hands toward body and then push out spreading arms until they extend to each side of the body.

STEP 6 (photo 6) Relax wrists so that hands drop and rotate them forward so that palms face upward.

STEP 7 (photo 7) Draw arms back to the front of the body.

STEP 8 (photo 8-9) Bend elbows to bring hands toward body. Then rotate wrists back and inward until palms face downward.

STEP 9 (photo 10) Lightly press hands down toward knees. Again first touch fingertips to the knees, then relax arms so that hands come to rest on knees.

STEP 10 (photo 11) Turn fingers slightly inward and circle the hands out and back to a position in front of the stomach. Wrists are relaxed with fingers pointing down, and the right hand is behind the left. Rotate hands so that palms are up, and right hand is above the left. Allow hands to sink to the lap. You should be back at the meditative position.

9

10

11

12

FORM II Lighting the Back Burning Spaces

STEP 1 (photo 1-6a) The beginning of this form is a repetition of steps 1-5 of Form I; except do not stop spreading arms when they extend to each side of the body. Instead, continue moving them back and downward.

STEP 2 (photo 7) Draw hands up along the side of the body with palms facing rearward until they reach a position halfway up the back. Then, turn hands inward so that palms and fingers are against the back.

5

6

6A

7

79

STEP 3 (photo 8 & 9) Slide both hands down over the lower back all the way to the floor until the backs of hands rest on the floor with fingers pointing toward each other. Rotate hands outward so fingers point straight back.

STEP 5 (photo 10) Simultaneously draw hands up, out, and forward until they extend to each side of the body at shoulder height. This movement is done with the hands trailing behind the wrists.

STEP 4 (photo 7-9) Repeat steps 2 and 3 two more times, but the last time, hands slide to the floor; do not rotate them.

8

9

10

STEP 6 (photo 11-13) The rest of this form is a repeat of steps 6-10 of Form I.

11

12

13

FORM III   Extending the Wings & Twisting the Neck

STEP 1 (photo 1-5) Repeat steps 1-5 of Form I.

STEP 2 (photo 6-8) Arms should now be extended at shoulder height to each side of the body. Palms are down. Turn head to the left and look at the tip of the middle finger. (Count thirty-six) Turn head back to center. (Count nine)
Turn head to the right and look at the tip of the middle finger. (Count thirty-six)
Turn head back to center

5

6

7

8

STEP 3 (photo 9-11) Repeat steps 6-10 of Form I.

STEP 4 (photo 12-14) Turn head to right. (Count thirty-six)
Turn head to center. (Count nine)
Turn head to left. (Count thirty-six)
Turn head back to center.

13

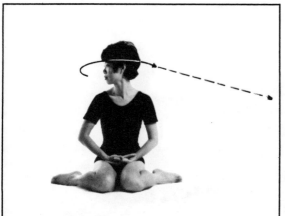

14

FORM IV Holding the Warm Jade Pillow

STEP 1 (photo 1) Push hands straight out, simultaneously spreading them apart, and slightly tilting them back. Eyes should look between middle fingers.

STEP 3 (photo 3) Move hands back and down behind neck where fingers are interlocked. The head is simultaneously bent completely forward.

STEP 2 (photo 2) Move hands up and back in an arc. During this movement, eyes continue looking between middle fingers while head correspondingly tilts back until it and hands are at a 65° angle. (Count nine)

STEP 4 (photo 4 & 5) While bringing hands slightly forward, bend head back until it presses against the palms of the hands. (Count nine) As the hands are pushed slightly back, bend head all the way forward again. (Count nine) Repeat this eight more times. Bring hands up and forward over the top of the head while separating fingers. Simultaneously, lift head up so that it faces forward.

1

2

3

4

STEP 5 (photo 6 & 7) Lower hands toward knees. Just before hands reach knees, rotate them so that fingers are down. Touch fingertips to knees and then allow hands and arms to sink down so hands come to rest on knees.

STEP 6 (photo 8) Bend head back until it faces directly above. (Count thirty-six) Bend head forward again and when eyes are looking even with the knees; begin drawing hands back over the top of the thighs. At the same time, the head continues bending downward. When hands are near the stomach, the right hand passes behind the left. Turn hands so that palms face upward, and the right hand is on top. Allow hands to sink into lap and look at the center of the right palm. (Count thirty-six)

5

6

7

8

STEP 7 (photo 9) Lift head back to the starting position.

9

FORM V Sounding the Ancient Drums

STEP 1 (photo 1 & 2) Lean forward and rotate the body counter clockwise in a full circle. When body is leaning to the left, eyes should look to the left and concentrate on hearing with the left ear. When body begins to lean to the right, eyes should look to the right and concentrate on hearing with right ear. Repeat steps 1 and 2 of Form IV.

STEP 2 (photo 3) Lower head so that it faces straight forward while hands move back slightly until they are directly over the top of the head. Hands then move down and palms completely cover the ears.

1

2

3

4

STEP 3 (photo 4 & 4a) Place the tip of each index finger on top of each middle finger. Simultaneously bend index fingers, rubbing them against the tops and sides of middle fingers. Place the outer side of the top joint of each index finger against the neck and snap them against the neck to the extended position. Repeat this step 23 more times. Bring hands up and then forward.

STEP 4 (photo 5 & 6) Repeat step 5 of Form IV.

STEP 5 (photo 7) Lean forward and rotate body clockwise in a full circle. When body leans to the right, eyes look to the right and concentrate on hearing with the right ear. When the body leans to the left, eyes look to the left and concentrate on hearing with the left ear. Repeat Step 10 of Form I.

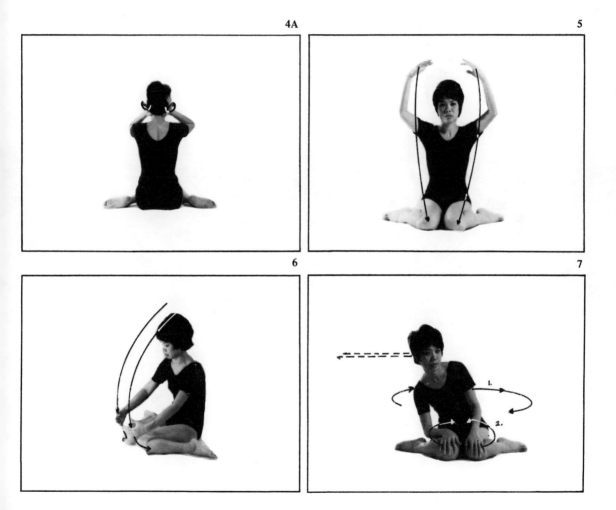

4A

5

6

7

8

FORM VI Chewing with Both Wings Upward

STEP 1 (photo 1-3) Keeping mouth closed, exercise jaws by biting down and stretching them apart repeatedly for 36 times. (Swallow the saliva each time the jaws bite down) This is done while the head turns all the way to the left, then all the way to the right and back to center. Push hands straight out while spreading them apart. Lift hands and arms to shoulder height while rotating hands so that fingers point out and palms are up. (count thirty-six)

STEP 2 (photo 4) Spread arms apart until they are extended to either side of the body.

1   2   3   4

STEP 3 (photo 5-7) Turn head to the left and look at the middle finger. (count thirty-six) Turn head back to the center. (count nine)
Turn head to the right and look at the middle finger. (count thirty-six) Turn head back to the center. Draw arms back to the front of the body. (count thirty-six)

STEP 4 Repeat steps 8 to 10 of Form I.

5

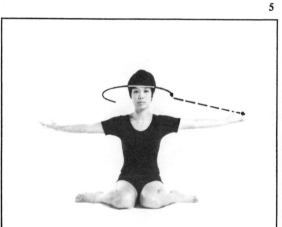

6

7

94

The Gracful Pheonix (taking the legs out)

STEP 1 (photo 1 & 2) Lean slightly to the left, right then back to the center. Raise the right hand, palm up, to shoulder height. Turn the palm in. The right hand circles forward while the left hand is raised to shoulder height. The left hand rotates so that the palm faces outward. Simultaneously, the right hand circles back under the left hand to a position above the right shoulder, the left hand circles out past the left knee and the right leg is raised.

STEP 2 (photo 3, 4, 4a) Push right hand forward while extending right leg. Simultaneously the left hand is drawn back to a point out from the left hip. Lean forward and bend the right hand down so fingers point straight ahead.

1

2

3

4

95

STEP 3 (photo 5) Still bending forward, the right arm and body sweep to the left.

STEP 4 (photo 5 & 6) As the body resumes its erect posture, the left arm bends in front of the shoulders, and the right arm bends back under it. The left hand circles forward, then under the right hand, and back above the left shoulder. Simultaneously, the right hand circles back, up, and out past the right knee while the left leg is raised.

4A

5

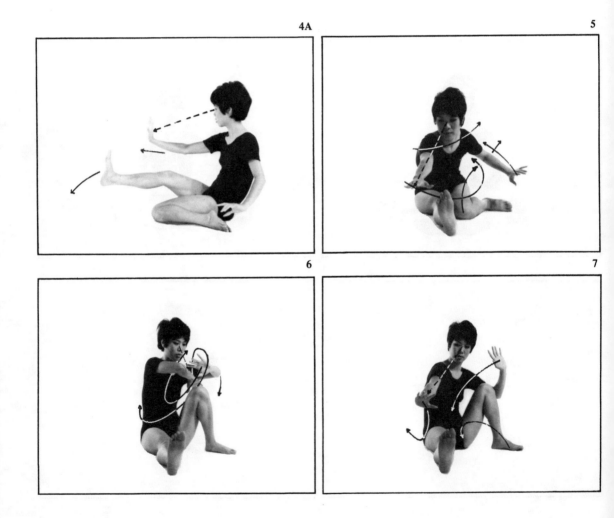

6

7

STEP 5 (photo 7 & 7a) Push left hand forward while extending left leg. Simultaneously, the right hand is drawn back beside the right hip. Lean forward and bend the left hand down so that fingers point straight ahead.

STEP 6 (photo 8) The body resumes its erect posture as the left hand is drawn back beside the left hip.

7A

8

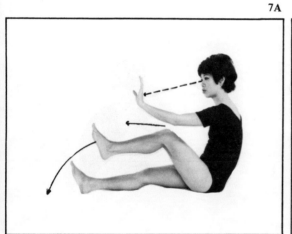

FORM VII   Circling the Heavens

STEP 1 (photo 1) Bring hands above legs while pushing them forward until the fingers touch toes. Head is erect. (count nine)

STEP 2 (photo 2-4) Rotate hands outward, lower them and bring them back along the side of the legs. When they reach the hips, rotate them inward until fingers face the rear.

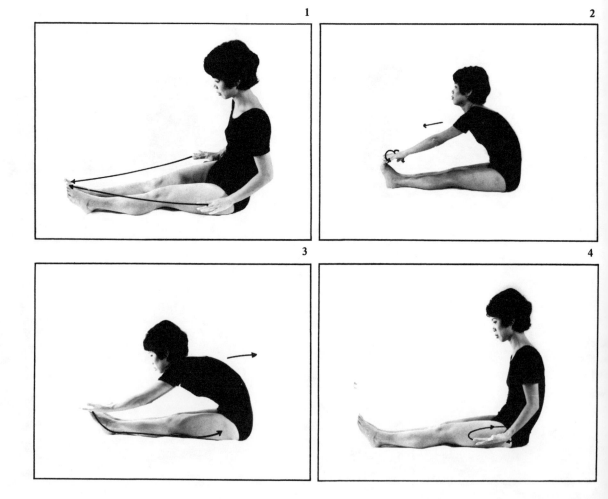

STEP 3 (photo 5) Lift hands up until they are in front of the shoulders

STEP 5 (photo 7 & 8) Release hands and rotate them outward so that palms are up. Bring hands back along the sides of legs while straightening the body. When they pass the knees, circle them outward and fold them in so that palms are down.

STEP 4 (photo 6) Push hands toward feet while bending body forward. Hands hold the feet while the head rests on the legs slightly below the knees. (count nine)

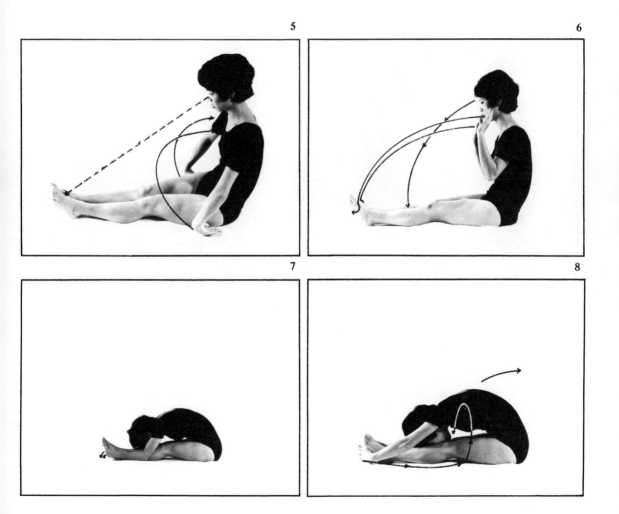

5

6

7

8

9

FORM VIII Polishing the Wheels

STEP 1 (photo 1) Bending elbow, bring right hand across the chest. Life right leg and then simultaneously sweep the right arm and leg 90° to the right. Bend left forearm across the chest.

STEP 3 (photo 3) The body and arms sweep towards the left leg as the left arm is extended. While the right hand returns under the left armpit, the left hand again is brought back across the chest. The right hand circles across the face and to the right toes.

STEP 2 (photo 2) The right hand then circles down, under the left armpit, across the face, and down to the right knee.

STEP 4 (photo 4) Repeat step 3; except, after the right hand crosses the face, extend both hands to the right foot. Both hands hold the right foot with thumbs on top and fingers underneath. The left hand is below the right hand. The head is twisted so that its right side rests slightly below the knee of the right leg.

1

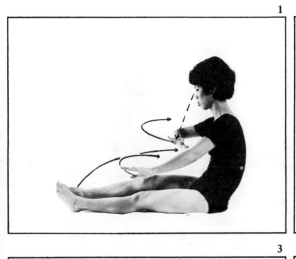

2

3

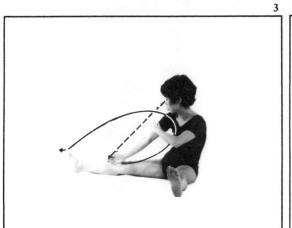

4

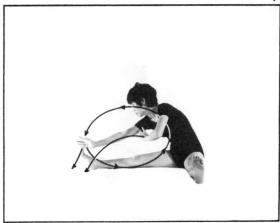

STEP 5 (photo 5-6) Release hands and lift body back up with the left hand coming under the right armpit. Bend the right elbow so that the right hand is across the chest and circle the left hand across the face and to the left knee.

STEP 7 (photo 8) Repeat step 6, except that both hands extend to hold the left foot with the right hand below the left. The left side of the head rests on the left leg slightly below the knee.

STEP 6 (photo 7) The body and arms sweep toward the right leg as the right arm is extended. While the left hand returns under the right armpit, the right hand again is brought back across the chest. The left hand circles across the face and to the left toes.

STEP 8 (photo 9-10) Release hands and lift body back up. At the same time, the left arm comes across the chest while the right arm sweeps towards the right leg and swings up behind the left. Separate the hands while bending down and touching the forehead to the floor. The left hand holds the left foot while the right hand holds the right.

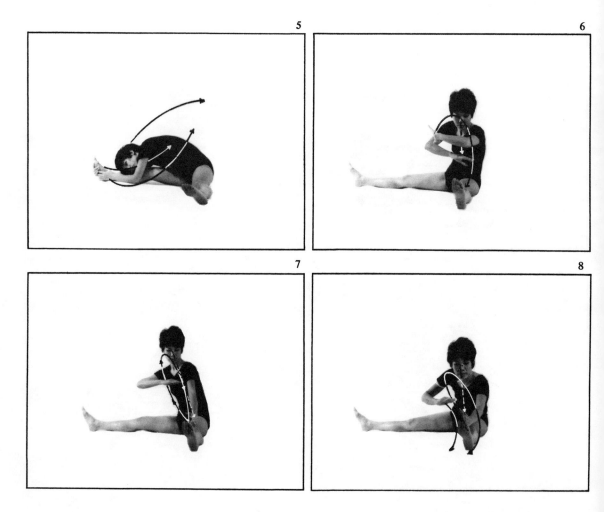

5

6

7

8

STEP 9 (photo 11) Lift the body back up. The left hand is brought across the chest and extended, palm up above the left leg while the right hand passes under the left armpit and stops in front of the left shoulder (palm down).

STEP 11 Sweep right arm and right leg 90° to the right. Bring the left hand across the face and extend it, palm up, above the left leg. Simultaneously, the right hand passes under the left armpit and in front of the left shoulder (palm down). Repeat Step 10.

STEP 10 (photo 12) Lift the left leg and bring it together with the right leg. The left hand remains above the left leg moves with it as it is brought to the right. Bend the left arm under the right arm simultaneously turning the left palm down.

STEP 12 Repeat step 11 two more times. Separate hands, palms down, to the sides of the hips. You should be facing the same direction as at the start.

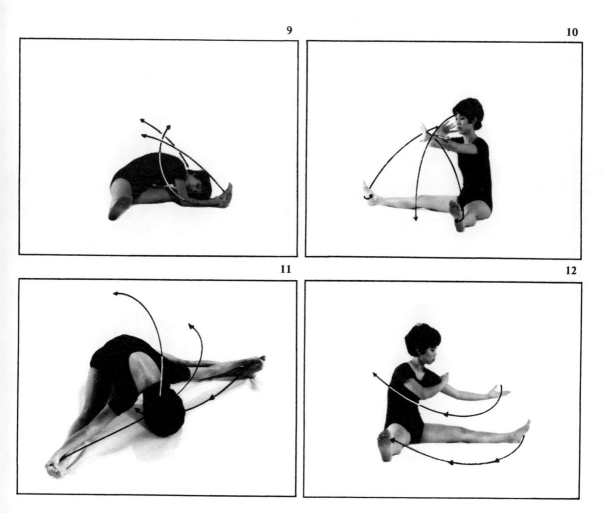

9

10

11

12

103

The Ascending Dragon (standing up)

STEP 1 (photo 1) Move right hand (palm down) in front of body. In a clockwise circle, move right hand to the right simultaneously sliding the right foot behind as in the meditative position. When the right hand completes the circle, extend the right arm (palm up).

STEP 3 (photo 3) Shifting the weight to the left knee, move the left foot back and out to assume the meditative position. At the same time, move the left hand in a clockwise motion and the right hand in a counterclockwise motion to end with both hands (palms down) above the knees.

STEP 2 (photo 2) Sweep the right hand across body towards the left foot slowly turning the palm downwards. Simultaneously, bend the left arm across the chest, bend the right arm under it and place the sole of the left foot against the right thigh. Circle the hands (left moving forward, down, and back, and the right moving back, up and forward) until the left hand is behind the right, then extend the left arm (palm up) and lower the right hand (palm down) to the right hip.

STEP 4 (photo 4) Simultaneously, shift to the left, bend the left arm across the chest, move the right hand to the left, and bend the right arm to bring the right hand under and behind the left. Shift to the right, while extending the left arm

1

2

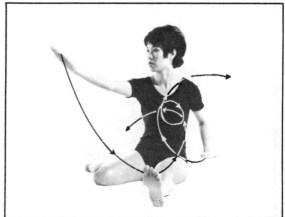

3

4

STEP 4 (photo 4) and the left leg to the left side and extending the right arm to the upper right. (Count three) Only the inside of the left foot will be on the floor.

STEP 6 (photo 6a) Bring the right hand down as you lean to the front on the right leg. At the same time, the right hand is lowered, and the left hand moves slowly to the right side of the body.

STEP 5 (photo 5-6) Place the left knee on the floor and slide the left foot back. Simultaneously shift the body on the left leg, (ower right hand) bend the left arm across the chest, move the right hand to the left, and bend the right arm to bring the right hand under and behind the left. Place the right foot to the front right in relation to the left knee. Slightly raise the body by kneeling on the left knee. At the same time, extend the right hand to the upper right and the left hand to the lower left. (Count three) As the hands are being extended, first look at the middle knuckle of the left hand and then turn the head to look at the middle knuckle of the right hand.

5

6

6A

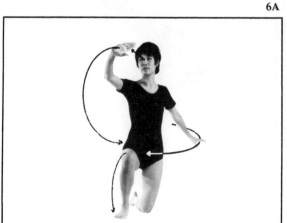

7

STEP 7 (photo 7-11) When executing the following movements, gradually stand up. Shift to the left, to the right, and back to the left. When moving to the left, the left hand sweeps across the face (from right to left), and when moving to the right, the right hand sweeps across the face, (from left to right). After moving to the left for the second time stop with the left hand to the upper left and the right hand to the lower right. (photo 10) (Count three). Lower the left hand while bringing the right hand to the left side of the body. Using the same hand movements, shift to the right, to the left, and back to the right. End with the right hand to the upper right and the left hand to the lower left. (photo 11) (Count three).

8

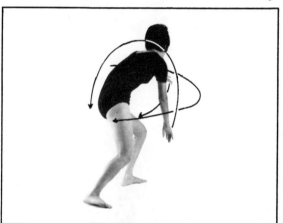

9

10

11

STEP 8 (photo 11-14) Lower the right hand while moving the left hand to the right side of the body. Sweep the left hand across the face in a counter-clockwise direction while shifting the weight to the left leg. Sweep the right hand across the face in a clockwise direction while shifting the weight to the right leg.

107

STEP 10 (photo 16-18) Lower the right hand while bringing the left hand to the right side of the body. Sweep the left hand across the face in a counter clockwise direction while shifting the weight to the left leg. Sweep the right hand across the face in a clockwise direction while shifting the weight to the right.

STEP 9 (photo 15, 15a) Lifting the hands up (palms up), raise the left foot.. Move the hands in small circles until palms are forward. Spreading the hands out to the sides, extend the left foot out to the side, then place it down. Simultaneously, turn to the right, raise the right hand to the upper right, and lower the left hand to the lower left. (Count three)

16

15A

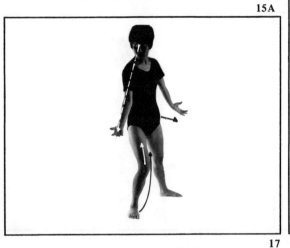

17

18

108

19

STEP 11 (photo 19-20a) Shift weight to the left foot. Use the same motions as in step 9, but with the right foot instead of the left. After placing the right foot down, simultaneously, shift the weight to the right, raise the right hand to the upper right, and lower the left hand to the lower left. (Count three)

20

20A

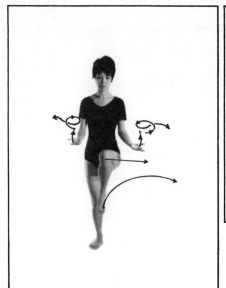

21

STEP 12 (photo 21-24) Simultaneously lower the right hand and extend the left hand to the right. Shift the weight to the left leg while extending the right hand to the left. Move back to the center and distribute the weight evenly to both legs. At the same time, allow the right forearm to move behind the left forearm so that they are crossed. Separate hands and lower them to the sides. Lift the left foot and place it down beside the right foot while forming fists, thumbs inside, with the hands.

22

23

24

110

Instructions for the Eight Silken Forms in the standing Positions

Preliminary Instructions

The starting position for the standing forms is feet together, arms at the sides and hands formi.g loose fists with the thumbs inside. The description for each of the forms ends with the form being closed; that is, ending in the starting position. If one chooses to practice the forms continuously, it is not necessary to bring the left foot beside the right and form fists, thumbs inside, with the hands. Instead, leave the feet apart and when the hands return to the sides, begin the next form. The last form, Welling the Life Root, is an exception because it begins with the feet together, but it poses no problem because the preceding form, The Gentle Fist, ends with the feet together.

The knees should always be bent slightly, and when the body is lowered, this is accomplished by bending at the knees.

Employ "reversed breathing" at all times. Exhale when raising arms and when hands push out. When the hands move back, inhale. Also, when the hands make a change the breathing also changes. These are just some general rules to keep in mind. With practice one will be able to feel when his breathing is properly coordinated with the movements.

Preliminary

STEP 1 Lift left foot and take a step laterally to the left. At the same time, open hands and allow them to hang loose at sides.

1

STEP 2 (photo 1) Raise hands to stomach height. Bend arms to bring hands towards the body. Fingertips face each other, and palms are down. Tracing nearly a full circle, move hands forward, down, and back towards the body. The hands come to rest, palms down, slightly below the navel.

2

3

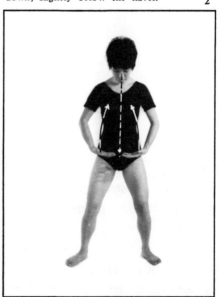

4

STEP 3 (photo 2) Lift hands straight up until they reach the middle of the chest.

STEP 5 (photo 5) Lightly push hands down until they are at navel level. Rotate hands so that fingers point forward.

STEP 4 (photo 3 & 4) Tracing nearly a full circle, move hands forward, up, and back ending with the hands, palms down, at shoulder height.

STEP 6 (photo 6) Push hands forward and circle them out and down to the sides of the body where they form fists with the thumbs inside. As the hands circle down to the sides lift the left foot and place it down beside the right foot.

5

6

Supporting Heaven With Both Hands

STEP 1 Repeat Step 1 of the Preliminary

STEP 2 (photo 1) Rotate hands so that palms face inward. Raise arms to the sides all the way until the hands are above the head. Interlock fingers.

STEP 2 (photo 2) Lower hands until they touch the head and then push them up. Repeat this two more times.

1

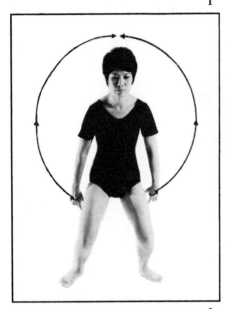

2

3

4

STEP 3 (photo 3-6) Turn palms forward and disengage the fingers. Turn palms down and lower hands in front of face; continue pushing down and conclude as in the preliminary.

5

6

Pointing Out The Eagle

STEP 1 Repeat Step 1 of the Preliminary.

STEP 2 (photo 1) Raise hands forward to shoulder height.

STEP 4 (photo 3 & 4) Push the right hand across the body and under the left arm while shifting the weight to the left leg.

STEP 3 (photo 2) Shift weight to the left leg and then shift weight to the right leg while drawing the right hand back.

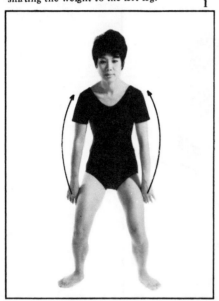

1

2

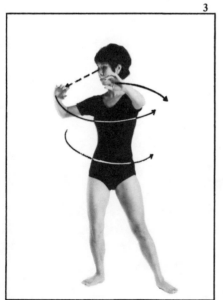

3

4

STEP 5 (photo 5) Bend left arm and rotate body to the right while extending the right arm out and to the right in a sweeping motion. Shift weight to the right leg.

STEP 7 (photo 7) Lower the right hand under the left arm while lowering the body by bending the knees. Move arms and body as in step 5.

STEP 9 (photo 9) Raise body to its original height. Lower right hand under the left arm and again repeat the arm and body movements of step 5.

STEP 6 (photo 6) Lower the left hand under the right arm. Bend the right arm and rotate the body to the left while extending the left arm out and to the left in a sweeping motion. Shift weight to the left leg.

STEP 8 (photo 8) Lower the left hand under the right arm while the body is lowered further. Move arms and body as in step 6.

5

6

7

8

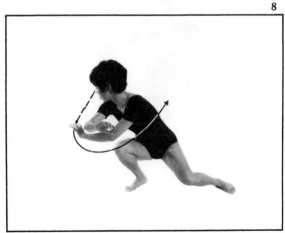

STEP 10 (photo 10) Lower left hand under right arm while bending the right arm until the right hand, palm out, is in front of the face. Turn back to the center, shift the weight to the left leg, rotate the right hand so that the palm is down, and lower it towards the left hand. At the same time, slightly raise the left hand while rotating it so the palm is up, and lift and right leg up. Both hands form fists.

STEP 11 (photo 11 & 12) Simultaneously, draw the left hand to the left side; step out with the right foot to the front right; and lift the right hand across the face, where the index and middle fingers are extended, and out above the right leg. The index and middle fingers should be vertical, and the tips of them at eye level. (Count nine).

9

10

11

12

STEP 12 (photo 13 & 14) Shift weight to the left leg and extend the right arm straight out. (Count three). Open right hand and rotate it until the palm is down. Rotate the body to the right until the right hand is to the rear center while the right hand is simultaneously lowered to waist level.

STEP 13 (photo 15) Rotate right hand so that the palm is up. (Count three) Turn back towards the front until the right hand, palm up is above the right leg.

STEP 14 (photo 16) Bring the right arm to the side of the body and form a fist while lifting the right foot and placing it down beside the left foot.

13

14

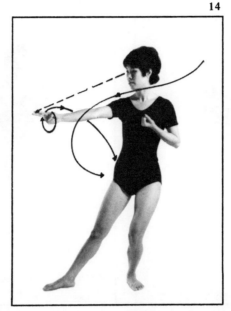

15

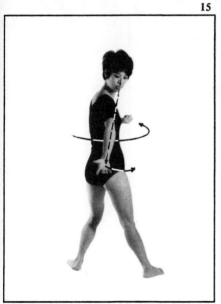

16

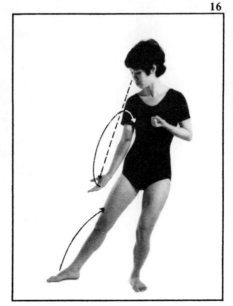

STEP 15 (photo 17 & 18) Rotate fists inward until palms are down and open them. Take a step laterally to the left with the left foot while spreading hands circularly out and to the sides.

STEP 16 (photo 19-26) The rest of this form is a repetition of the same movements on the opposite side. That is, after raising arms, shift weight to the right leg. Shift weight to the left leg while drawing the left hand back. Push left hand across the body and under the right arm while shifting the weight to the right leg, etc.

17

18

19

20

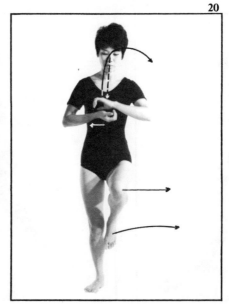

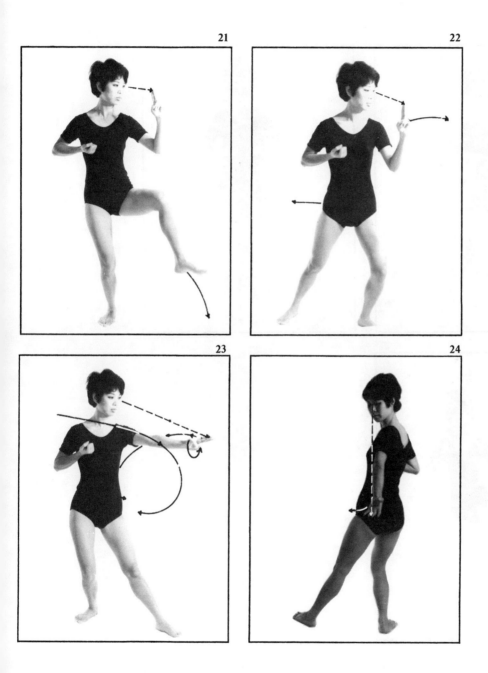

STEP 17 (photo 25-27) After bringing the left hand to the side of the body, forming a fist, while lifting the left foot and placing it down beside the right foot (photo 25); rotate hands inward until palms are down and open them. Then take a step laterally to the right with the right foot while spreading the hands circularly out and to the sides. To close the form, form fists with the thumbs inside while raising the left foot and placing it beside the right foot.

25

26

27

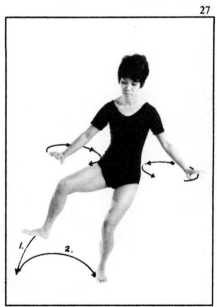

Reviewing The Four Quarters

STEP 1 Repeat Step 1 of the Preliminary.

STEP 2 (photo 1) Raise hands forward to shoulder height.

STEP 3 (photo 2) Shift weight to the left leg and then shift weight to the right leg while drawing the right hand back.

STEP 4 (photo 3 & 4) Push the right hand across the body and under the left arm while shifting the weight to the left leg.

1

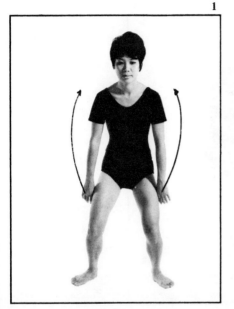

2

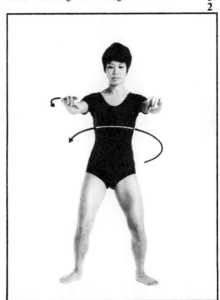

3

4

123

STEP 5 (photo 5) Bend left arm and rotate body to the right while extending the right arm out and to the right in a sweeping motion. Shift weight to the right leg. Continue moving the hands until the fingers are pointing to the right and upward. The right palm faces the front while the left palm faces the right elbow.

STEP 6 (photo 6) Press the hands forward and then rotate them in circles until the wrists are down. (The right hand is rotated counter clockwise while the left hand is rotated clockwise)

STEP 7 (photo 7) Draw the left hnd back as far as the left shoulder and lower it slightly while shifting weight to the left leg.

5

6

7

8

124

STEP 8 (photo 8 & 9) Push left hand across the body and under the right arm while shifting weight back to the right leg. Bend the right arm and rotate body to the left while extending the left arm out and to the left in a sweeping motion. Shift weight to the left leg. Continue moving hands until fingers are pointing to the left and upwards. The left palm faces the front while the right palm faces the left elbow.

STEP 9 (photo 10) Press hands forward and then rotate them in circles until palms are down. (The right hand is rotated counter clockwise while the left hand is rotated clockwise).

STEP 10 (photo 11) Draw right hand back as far as the right shoulder and lower it slightly while shifting weight to the right leg.

9

10

11

12

STEP 11 (photo 12 & 12a) Push right hand across the body and under the left arm while shifting weight to the left leg. Continue the same movements until having turned to the right three times. On the third time, after pushing the left hand under the right arm, bend the right arm until the right hand, palm forward is in front of the face.

STEP 12 (photo 13) Turn to the center and shift the weight to the left leg. Rotate the right hand until the palm is down and lower it to shoulder level. At the same time, rotate left hand until the palm is up, and raise it until it almost touches the right hand.

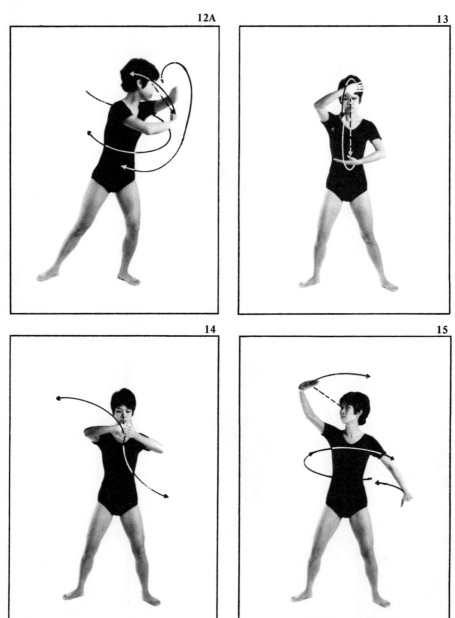

STEP 13 (photo 14) Pull hands apart and simultaneously raise the right hand, palm out, to the upper right; lower the left hand, palm down, near the left hip; and shift the weight to the right leg. Look at the middle knuckle of the right hand. (count three)

STEP 14 (photo 15) Shifting weight to the left leg, rotate body until it faces directly left. (count three)

STEP 15 (photo 16) Rotate the right foot on its ball 90° to the left. Turn body until it faces the rear. (Count three)

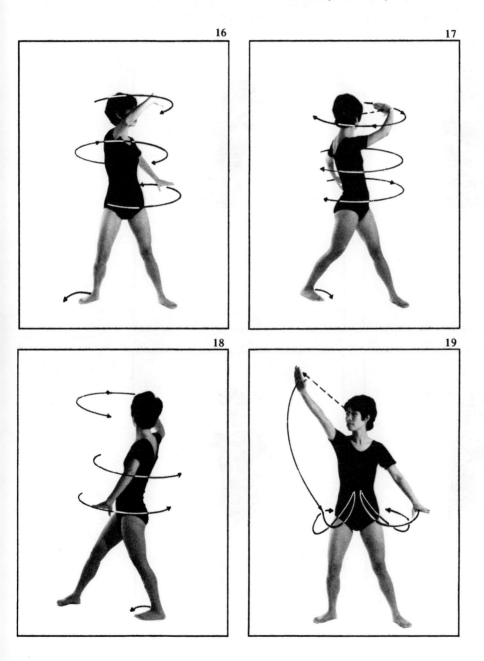

16

17

18

19

127

STEP 16 (photo 17) Begin turning back to the front until the body again faces directly left. (Count three) Turn body back to the front while the right foot is gradually rotated, again on the ball of the foot, to its original position. Shift weight to the right leg as the body is rotated until it faces directly right. (Count three) Use the ball of the left foot to rotate it 90° to the right. Continue turning

the body until it faces the rear. (Count three)

STEP 17 (photo 18) Turn back towards the front and pause when the body faces directly right. (count three) Turn body back to the front while the left foot is gradually rotated, again on the ball of the foot, to its original position. The weight should again be distributed evenly.

20

21

22

23

STEP 19 (photo 20-27) The rest of this form is a repetition of the same movements on the opposite side. That is, after raising the arms, shift the weight to the right leg. Shift the weight to the left leg while drawing the left hand back. Push the left hand across the body and under the right arm while shifting weight to the right leg, etc. After lowering the left hand near the left hip and at the same level as the right hand, (photo 27), bring both hands in front of the body at waist level, and conclude as in the Preliminary.

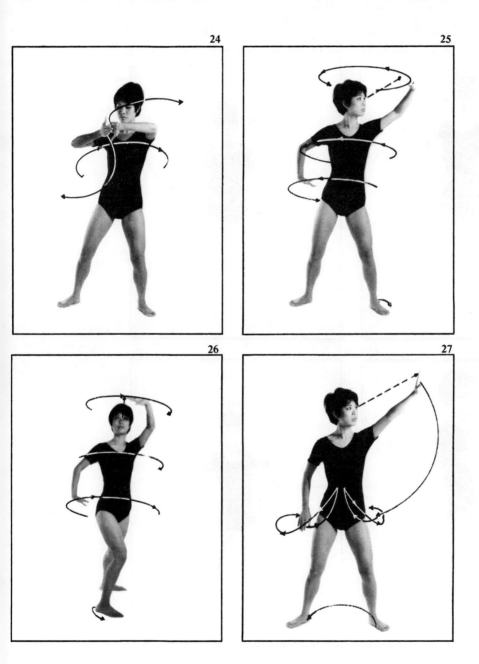

24

25

26

27

Forming The Force

STEP 1 Repeat step 1 of the Preliminary.

STEP 2 (photo 1) Raise the hands along each side of the body (thumbs inward). Reaching the bottom of the rib cage, turn both hands palms up (fingers forward) while slightly sliding them forward. The middle of each forearm is against each side of the body, and fingers point slightly inward. **1**

STEP 3 (photo 2 & 2a) Extend the hands straight out. Separate the arms to the sides of the body.

STEP 4 (photo 3) Place the weight on the right leg, simultaneously turning the body to the left. **2**

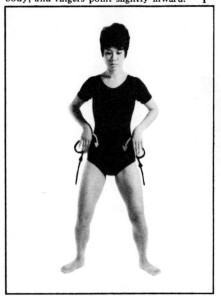

2A

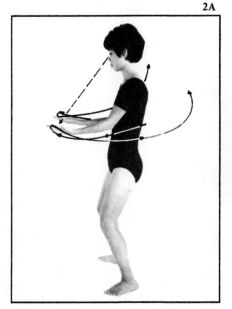

3

STEP 5 (photo 4 & 5) Distribute weight to the left leg and turn to the right while the right hand is gradually lowered and the left hand is gradually raised above and in front of the head. While turning, the weight should be distributed to the right leg.

STEP 6 (photo 6) When the right hand is at the side of the right hip and the left hand in line with the center of the face, lower the left hand straight down and simultaneously begin to raise the right hand. Concentrate on the finger tip of the left hand's middle finger. When finger tips are at eye level, move the left elbow out to the side while the left hand (palm down) is in front of the face.

4

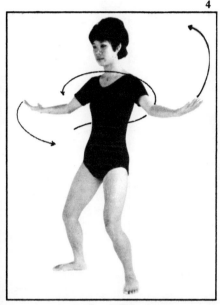

5

6

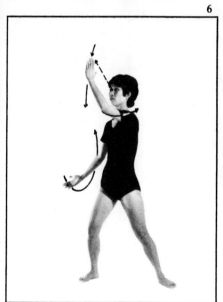

7

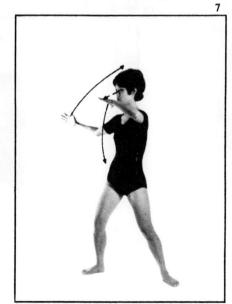

STEP 7 (photo 7-10) Lower the left hand in a pressing motion for about 3 inches, then continue lowering the hand while raising the right hand. Simultanrously, turn the body towards the left, gradually lower the left hand, and raise the right hand above and in front of the head. Concentrate on the middle knuckle of the left hand. Slowly distribute the weight to the left leg.

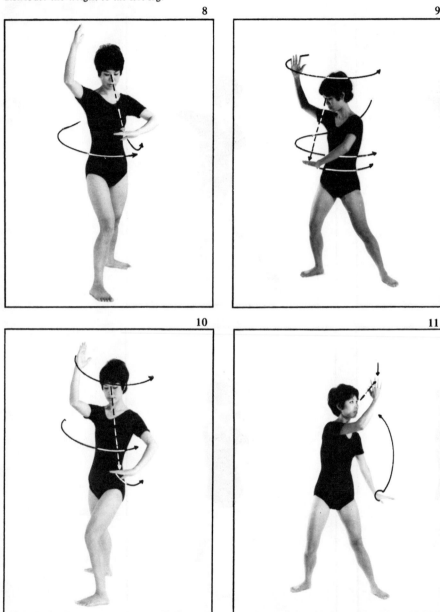

8

9

10

11

STEP 8 (photo 11-16) When the right hand is in line with the center of the face and the left hand reaches the side of the left hip, rotate the left hand so that the palm is up. Repeat movements as on the right side. This sequence of movements is done 3 times on each side. During the third time on the left side, keep the left palm facing down. Turn to the front while lowering the right hand to the right side at the same level as the left hand (both palms are down).

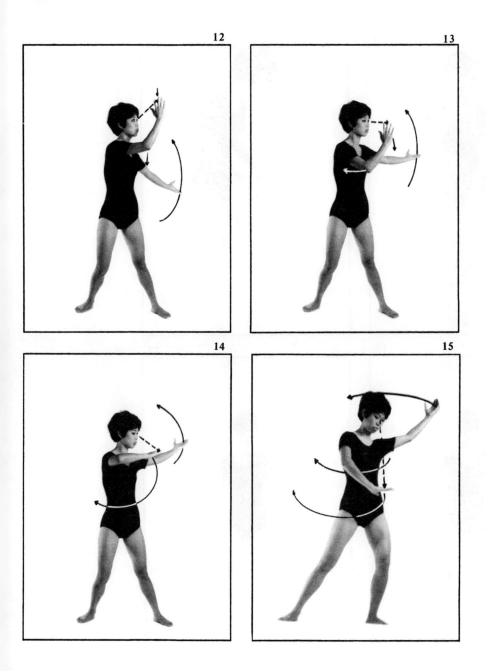

STEP 9 (photo 17-21) Relax the wrists so fingers point down and raise hands in front of the waist. Lift hands so palms are down and push them forward and out in a circular motion until they come back in front of the body. Raise both hands in front of the body until they reach the bottom of the rib cage. Turn both hands palms up (fingers forward) while slightly sliding them forward. The middle of each forearm is against each side of the body, and fingers point slightly inward. Extend the hands straight out.

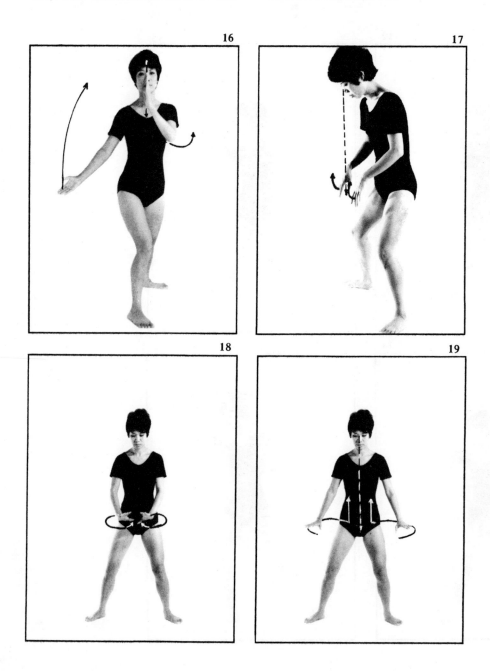

STEP 10 Repeat the same movements as in steps 3-8, but the movements will now alternate to the opposite side of the body. That is, instead of initially moving to the left, the initial turning is to the right, instead of lowering the right hand and raising the left, the left hand is lowered and the right raised, etc.

STEP 11 (photo 22-24) To close the form, repeat step 9. Then bend the hands down at the wrists (fingers point down) and rotate them outward until the finger tips are up. Bend hands forward so that palms are down, and lower them to the sides. Lift the left foot and place it down beside the right foot while forming fists with thumbs inside.

20

21

22

23

135

24

Upon A Divine Horse

STEP 1 (photo 1-2a) Begin as in Step 1 of
the Preliminary; except, the stance is very
wide as if one is sitting on a horse. Raise
both hands forward to head level. Imagine
that hands are holding up a large pole. Lower
hands forward while bending the knees to
lower body. Place hands on knees.

1

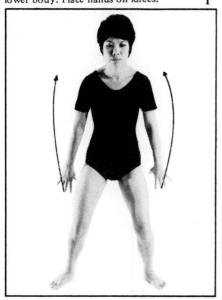

2

2A

3

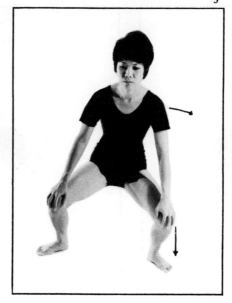

STEP 2 (photo 3-5) Lean to the left and look to the front left. Lean to the right and look to the front right. Release hands and bend over the right leg.

STEP 3 (photo 6-7) Shift weight to the left leg while moving the hands to the left. Look at the middle knuckle of the right hand while using it to push to the left until it is under the left arm. Bend left arm and extend the right arm out and to the right in a sweeping motion while rotating the body and shifting the weight to the right leg.

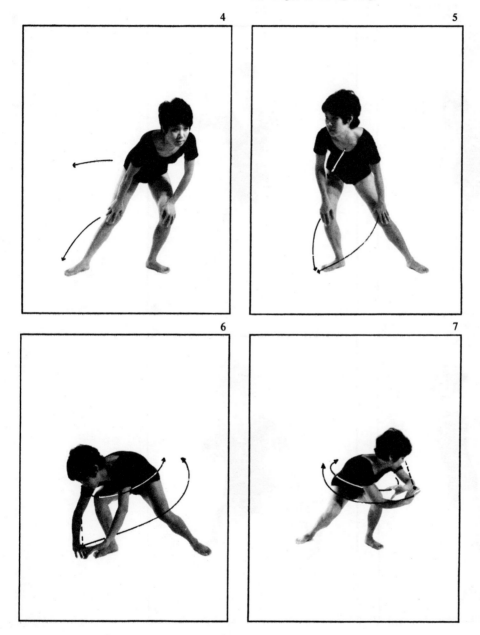

4

5

6

7

STEP 4 (photo 8) Turn both palms face up and lower left hand so that it is now under the right arm. Bend the right arm and extend the left arm out and to the left in a sweeping motion while rotating body and shifting weight to the left leg.

STEP 5 (photo 9 & 10) Turn both palms to face out and lower right hand under the left arm. Continue the same movements as above. As the movement to each side is executed, gradually stand up. After having turned to the right 3 times, turn to the center.

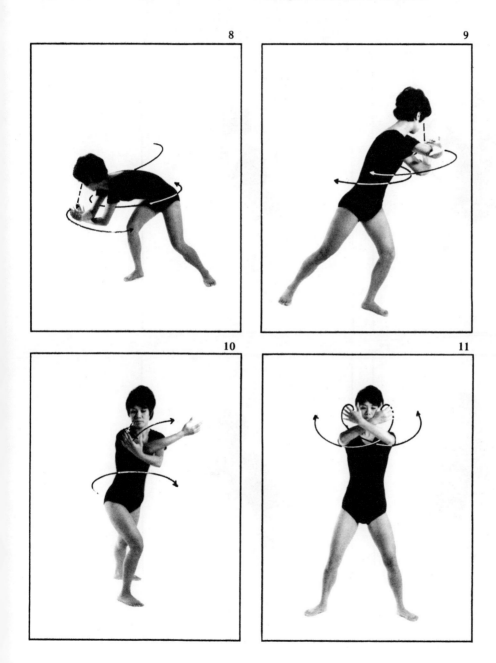

8

9

10

11

STEP 6 (photo 11) At this point, you should be standing with knees slightly flexed and both arms should be crossed (right behind the left) with palms facing inward. The weight should be evenly distributed. Fold arms inward until both palms face forward, and left arm is behind the right arm. Separate hands.

STEP 7 (photo 12-16) Shift weight to the left leg while slightly drawing the left hand back. Shift weight to the right leg while pushing the left hand under the right arm. Repeat hand and body movements as in steps 3-5; except, when moving to the left, the right palm is down and the left palm is out; when moving to the right, both palms are up; and while executing the movements, the body is gradually lowered. After having turned to the left 3 times, turn to the center.

12

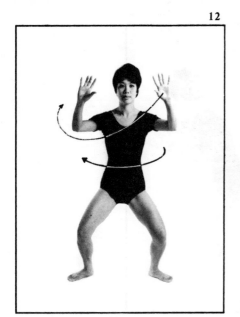

13

14

15

140

STEP 8 (photo 17) Arms should be crossed with the left arm behind the right arm, and weight is evenly distributed. Separate hands and place them on knees. Repeat step 2.

STEP 9 (photo 18-20) Move to the center while standing up raising hands, and holding them out as in the beginning pose. Lower hands to the side and place left foot next to the right foot while forming fists (thumbs inside) with the hands.

16

17

18

19

20

The Gentle Fist

STEP 1 (photo 1, 2) Repeat step 1 of the Preliminary and then raise hands palms up to the bottom of the rib cage while forming fists. Rotate fists until knuckles face out while lowering arms slightly. Raise arms in forward to shoulder height.

STEP 2 (photo 3) Shift weight to left leg, then to the right leg while drawing the right fist back. Distribute weight to the left. Simultaneously, push right fist across the body and under the left arm.

1

2

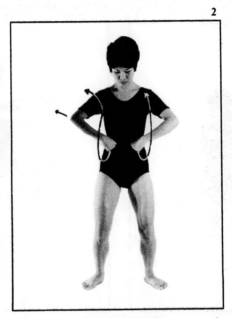

3

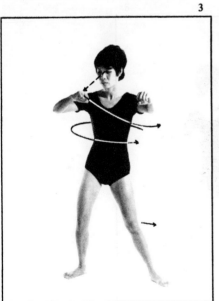

4

STEP 3 (photo 4, 5) Turn to the right using the same arm and body movements as in "Pointing Out the Eagle." After turning to the right and shifting weight to the right leg, continue to move the right fist a little further. Rotate both fists so that the knuckles are down. Draw the left fist to the center of the body while moving the right arm in a counter clockwise circle until both fists come together at the center of the body (left fist's knuckles

down and right fist's knuckles up). At the same time shift the weight to the left leg while lifting the right leg.

STEP 4 (photo 6 & 7) Step out to the front right with the right foot and shift weight to the right leg. Simultaneously, draw the left fist to the left side while bringing the right fist in front of the right shoulder and extending it (knuckles up) above the right leg in a punching motion.

5

6

7

8

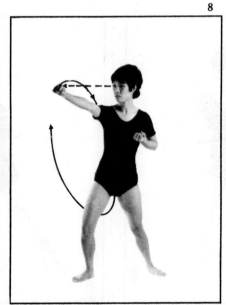

144

STEP 5 (photo 8) Keeping weight on the right leg, sweep the right fist back, down, and forward until it is at shoulder height (knuckles down).

STEP 6 (photo 9) Roll right arm in its shoulder socket. Step up with the left foot ending with the left heel against the instep of the right foot. At the same time, draw the right fist back until it is even with the left fist.

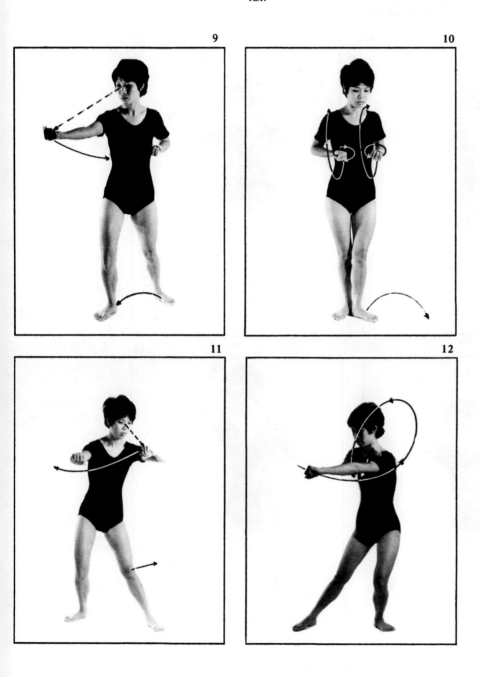

STEP 7 (photo 10-17) Simultaneously, step to the left with the left foot and rotate the fists until knuckles face out while lowering arms slightly. Raise arms forward to shoulder height and repeat the previous steps on the left side with the left fist. The entire sequence should be done a total of 4 times on each side. After the fourth time, with the left fist, rotate the fist until knuckles face up. Open hands, palms down, and lightly push hands down. Relax wrists so fingers point down.

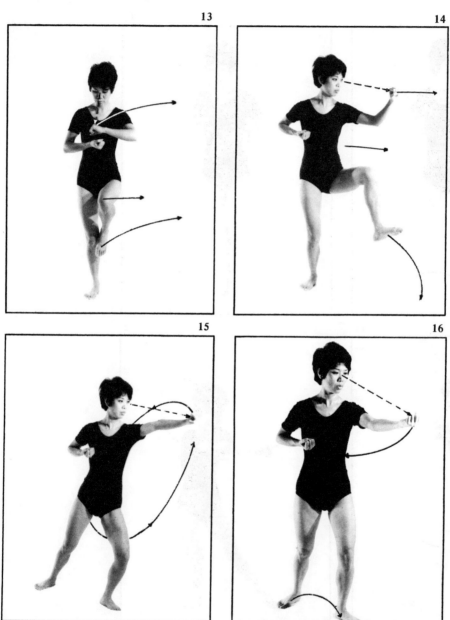

13

14

15

16

146

147

Welling The Life Root

STEP 1 (photo 1 & 2) Start with feet together and hands hanging at sides. Lift yourself off the floor with your toes while lifting hands (fingers down) to the bottom of the rib cage. Turn hands so that palms are facing down and lightly push down as you lower yourself. Relax wrists so fingers point down. Do this two more times.

STEP 2 (photo 2) Slowly bend forward and allow arms to hang down in front of the legs, touching fingertips to the floor. (Count thirty-six)

1

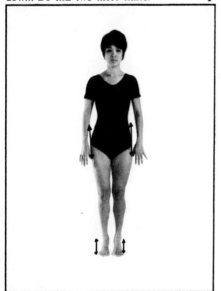

2

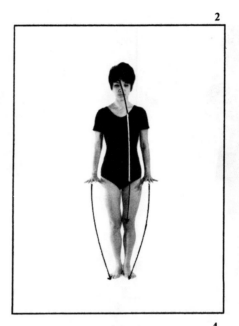

3

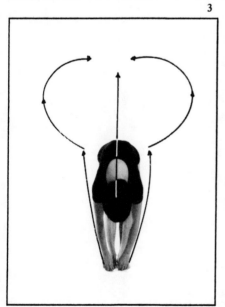

4

STEP 3 (photo 3) Slowly straighten up ending with hands hanging at the sides. Rotate hands until the palms face forward and raise arms out to the sides of the body ending with arms extended straight above the head. (palms facing forward) At the same time, tilt the head back and look between hands. (Count thirty-six)

STEP 4 (photo 4) Lower arms forward, correspondingly bending the head forward again. When arms reach shoulder level, begin bending forward and place both palms on the floor. (Count thirth-six)

STEP 5 (photo 5 & 5a) Slide hands back and grab ankles. (Count thirty-six)

5

5A

6

6A

STEP 6 (photo 6-7a) Release hands and slide them forward along the sides of the feet (backs of the hands touch the floor). Then straighten up the body, ending with the hands hanging at the sides.

STEP 7 (photo 8-10) Swing arms in a clockwise direction in front of the body. The right arm will create slightly more than a full circle while the left arm slightly more than a half-circle. (Begin Moving right arm first. When it has created half of its circle, begin moving the left arm.) End with the left arm behind the right arm. From this position, separate (right arm up and left arm down) and swing both arms to create one full clockwise circle with each arm. As arms are separated, the left foot should be taking a step to the left. When the right arm is beside

7

7A

8

9

the right leg, lift the right foot and place it down beside the left foot. Repeat this three more times.

STEP 8 (photo 11) At the end of the fourth swing, swing each arm in one full counter clockwise circle. End with the right arm behind the left arm.

STEP 9 (photo 12-14) Move to the right 4 times with the same motions but using a counter clockwise swing. After the fourth time, separate arms to the sides while taking a step laterally with the left foot. Raise hands out to the sides until they are above the shoulders (palms up).

10

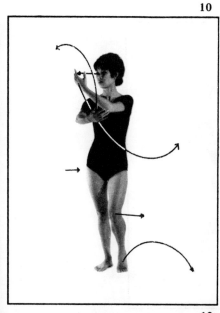

11

12

13

151

STEP 10 (photo 15 & 16) Simultaneously, bend knees and lower body, push up with arms, and tilt head back until looking straight up. Simultaneously, raise body, lower hands near the shoulders, and bend head forward until looking straight ahead. Do this two more times.

STEP 11 Close this form by pushing hands up slightly, moving them forward, and lowering them. Bring hands in front of waist, push them forward, and conclude as in the Preliminary.

14

15

16

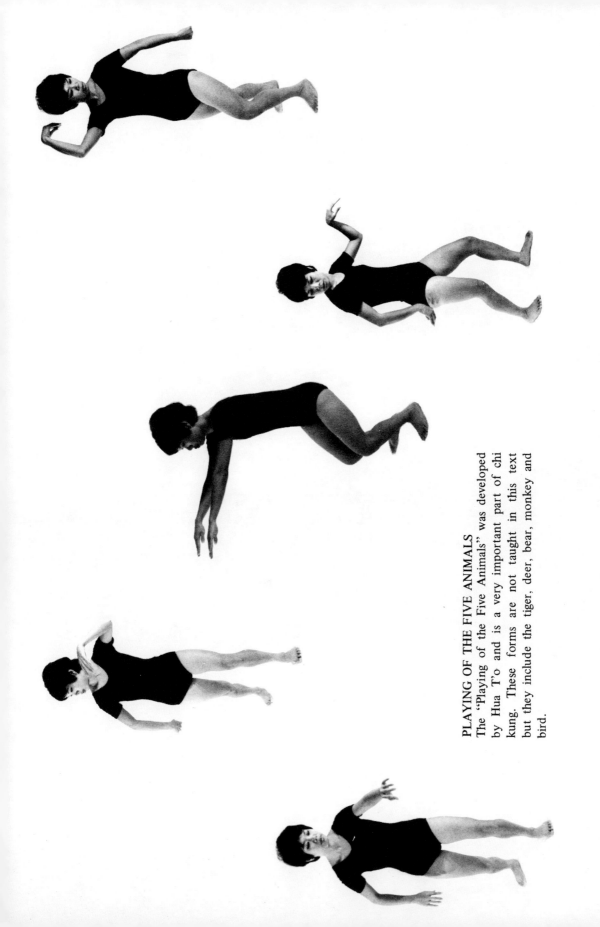

PLAYING OF THE FIVE ANIMALS
The "Playing of the Five Animals" was developed by Hua T'o and is a very important part of chi kung. These forms are not taught in this text but they include the tiger, deer, bear, monkey and bird.

Engrossed students listen to theory and philosophy behind
chi kung and each movement

With deep concentration students perform each movement.

159

As the mind flows so does the body.

In further study of ch'i, students learn acupuncture points.

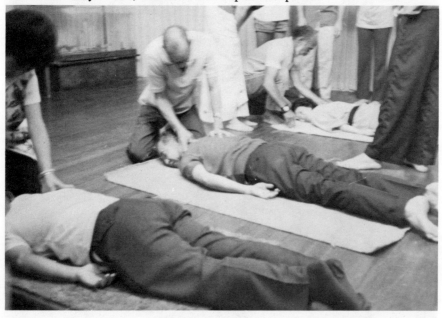

Some leading students display the beauty of ch'i kung.

On stage in chinatown, students delight a fascinated crowd.

Instruction not being limited to the classroom, students head to the mountains to get reacquainted with nature.

After a successful herb hunt students discuss their findings and further their understanding of the body.

Practicing in the woods amidst nature can be most stimulating.

Nature is brought amid solid concrete and the audience sits spellbound.

The arts of music and dance are culminated in this scene:

Dr. Siou takes time out to extend her understanding
personally to people.

Extending instruction further through TV, Dr. Siou
explains chi and acupuncture to Don Robbs.

Don Robbs and friends find out that there is much more
to chi kung than meets the eye.

After long serious study four students are acceptted
as disciples in a private ceremony.

The thumb print of each disciple is recorded.

With fascination Dr. Boylan and others learn of body energy.

The original class pose after a successful hunt for medicinal herbs.